THE CHURCH TRANSITION WORKBOOK

Getting Your Church in Gear

Bill Kemp

DISCIPLESHIP RESOURCES

PO BOX 340003 • NASHVILLE, TN 37203-0003
www.discipleshipresources.org

Cover and book design by Joey McNair

Edited by Linda R. Whited and Cindy S. Harris

ISBN 0-88177-422-7

Library of Congress Control Number 2004103785

DR422

Contents

Introduction

Who Is This Book For?

Every church is in a state of change. This book, though, is for those congregations who feel run over by change. Something has happened in the leadership of the church or in the community that has caused the members of the congregation to feel like road kill on the highway of faith. Perhaps conflict has left the church running on four flat tires. Or perhaps the congregation just feels stuck in the midst of a world that is moving too quickly. To move in a positive direction from such a state will require new energy, new vision, and a renewed trust in your church leadership.

Nothing less than a complete transformation is needed—a transition from the current state of congregational life to some other form of being the church. Transition is, in one sense, a passage or journey during which there may be the disorienting feeling of being neither here nor there. However, transition is also a rebirth in which there may be no choice but to experience radical change. The apostle John writes,

> Beloved, we are God's children now; what we
> will be has not yet been revealed. (1 John 3:2a)

There is a simple honesty to those words. They affirm that your congregational family is a child of God, given a unique place and identity in the grand scheme of God's kingdom. To make the transition from where you have landed to where you need to be will take faith, hope, and love—items that you already have. This book provides the other necessary ingredients: encouragement, another perspective, a supply of alternate road maps, and, above all, a process for working through your time of transition.

This book is for church leaders—both lay and clergy. One of the great mistakes of our era has been to provide clergy with a multitude of books, seminars, and other resources for church change, as if clergy could make things happen by themselves. Transition, however, is an organic process, meaning that it involves the whole congregation in a shift in activity and in self-understanding. Therefore, this book is written to be read by anyone who is concerned about the church's future. The contents are arranged to support some degree of participation by each member of the congregation.

How Is This Book to Be Used?

The contents of this book are particularly designed to foster group discussion and to be a shared resource for those church committees who find themselves riding herd on change. Who those committees are varies depending on the nature of the transition and the way the local church is organized. Ideally each member of the church's administrative council or governing board will read this book. Then the council can assign appropriate chapters to various committees and invite short-term study groups to work through its chapters. The idea is to percolate involvement in the process of transition down to the grass roots of the local congregation. This book, then, may be of particular benefit to

- any committee involved with pastoral relations or the search process for church employees or pastoral staff;

- the worship committee, because transition will inevitably affect when, where, and how the congregation worships;

- mission agencies or program boards, such as childcare programs or food banks. Although these groups are often separate entities, they are closely related to the church and will be affected by a transition process that reshapes the internal structure of the mission organization and the relationship the church has with its outreach ministries.

- witness work areas or evangelism committees, who may sense the need to lead their church to a more inviting relationship with their neighborhood;

- visioning groups or other short-term committees appointed to study the church's future and set goals. Take care, though. Remember that a token, small-group effort at understanding the process of transition is not the same as engaging the whole congregation in transformation.

This book lays down a framework for the process of change. It provides things to do when we feel stuck or when things feel unsettled. This book does not give a quick prescription for growth; rather, it is a guide to a transition process that enables us to weather change and come out with a renewed sense of mission and self-identity as a congregation.

This book is not designed to get everyone marching to the same drummer. Instead, it is a collection of resources organized around the developmental steps that are proven to promote healthy transition in local churches. You are invited to pick and choose what applies to your church.

To make the overall structure of these steps more obvious, the sections of the workbook have been given the names of an automotive transmission. As the congregation works through this transition process, you will sense the gears shifting as the church becomes unstuck and learns how to drive toward her destination.

Terms Used in This Book

Information for managing transition is provided for working in a variety of congregations and nonprofit agencies. Substitute the appropriate titles for your organization for each item.

Local Church or _____.
The terms *local church* and *church* refer to any organization that has a spiritual base. While *church* refers to the organizational unit, the complementary term *congregation* refers to the people, both members and visitors, who make up the worshiping fellowship. For nonprofit agencies, the congregation is the full group of both constituents, clients, and staff.

Church Council or _____.
The church council is the chief governing board of the local organization or congregation. This group usually meets monthly to handle a variety of issues and reports. This book will assume that the leadership and direction of this committee is in the hands of the laity.

Committee on Pastor/Staff-Parish Relations or _____.
This committee may be called personnel committee or search committee in some groups. This group works with any processes that relate to the relationship between staff, including a pastor, and the members of the congregation. It is this group that works with denominational leadership during a time of pastoral change and whenever there are issues that affect the congregation's relationship with employed staff. A period of transition thrusts additional tasks upon this group, which may need additional members and greater authority for this period.

Pastor or _____.
This person is the chief executive officer of the organization. Some churches may have multiple clergy, and the person with the greatest administrative portfolio is referred to as Senior Pastor. Other churches and mission agencies share an executive who may also have duties elsewhere.

District Superintendent or _____.
This is the denominational official who has direct oversight of the church or organization. This term is used to speak of the contact point the local congregation has with the wider church. Some organizations deal with an association or judicatory group that functions in this role rather than an individual.

Pilot Group or _____.
This name, borrowed from business transition sources, refers to the group who will work through the transition ideas presented in this book and discuss their implications for the whole congregation. This group may be an existing committee such as the committee on pastor/staff-parish relations or church council. It can also be a task force including the key leaders of the church formed just for the period of transition. The Pilot Group should read through at least Chapter 12 before the transition period is introduced as a concept to the congregation.

Understanding the Process

Tasks for Church Leaders in This Section

- Understand the nature of church trauma.

- Note the biblical material on transition for future study.

- Understand transition as a process that can be managed in steps.

- Decide whether to request special leadership for your church during transition.

Chapter 1
Transition and Trauma

Sometimes life in the church becomes painful. Remembering the day one of the families of the church left in a huff, we look over to the empty pew where they used to sit. A committee meets late into the night with the district superintendent discussing what we need next in a pastor. Is there, somewhere, a person who will come for the salary we pay, do what is needed, and miraculously placate the various factions in the church? In every aspect of the congregation's life, expectations and reality seem to be missing each other. Someone hits this nebulous nail on the head by saying, "Things are gonna have to change around here!"

Change is constant, both in the church and in life. Our usual response is to make small adjustments, minor course corrections. Only when our backs are up against the wall and circumstances feel out of control do we make dramatic alterations to our sense of identity and initiate dramatic shifts in direction. Years later, after the dust has settled, we can reflect and notice that the seeds for change were already planted long before the events that forced us to become a different person or church.

Traumatic events force a local church to change. Each crisis can be met with reluctance, bitterness, and self-pity; or it can be seen as an invitation to a period of transition. As we seek healing, we can discover new things about God and God's call upon the church. The transition process is an intentional response to traumatic events, but the ultimate goal of a transition process is to engage the church in a transformation that meets the challenges of the future. What the church shall become is never obvious, however, until the church finds healing for the pain it is currently experiencing. There are three general types of trauma being experienced by churches today:

1. **loss of or betrayal by pastoral leadership**

2. **conflict inside the church**

3. **neighborhood problems**

Each of these traumas has the potential to threaten the church's survival and force us to reevaluate our identity and mission. When these traumas come to a local church, it is useful for the congregation to declare an official period of transition. This declaration signals an end to the old game of fixing the blame and invites all the church leaders into an educational process of seeking new skills so that they can fix the problem together. By agreeing on a period of transition, the congregation gives themselves the time they need to walk the road of recovery. Seeking healing in this way is a faithful response to trauma.

Identify the forms of trauma that your own church has recently experienced. What in the descriptions that follow reminds you of horror stories you have heard about neighboring churches. Compare your notes with others. Then ask the "old-timers" of the congregation if there have ever been times like these in the past.

1. Loss of or Betrayal by Pastoral Leadership

Abuse of trust may take several forms.

- A beloved pastor dies or becomes disabled, leaving the church adrift—even following the installation of replacement clergy. Guilt that we have not done enough for this former pastor's memory or family may haunt the church members for years. No matter what the circumstances, the congregation may subconsciously blame themselves for somehow causing this loss. The lost pastor's pet programs or ways of doing things may be continued, even when they no longer fit the needs of the congregation. New pastors may feel as if they are walking on eggshells.

- A controlling pastor finally retires or moves to another parish, leaving the congregation without a sense of direction. This former pastor may have micromanaged church life, or he or she may simply have wielded such personal power that lay leadership no longer feels capable of directing church life. A power vacuum has resulted as competent lay leadership were gradually driven off and new people not trained. Those who remain feel ambivalent. They do not wish to yield so much power to the next pastor, but they do miss the former pastor's charisma. Any new leadership, lay or clergy, will be hard-pressed to meet everyone's expectations.

- There has been sexual or financial misconduct by a pastor or a prominent church leader. Unfortunately, such problems occur frequently enough that every congregation should be aware that they are at risk and should maintain rigorous policies to prevent abuse and to handle its consequences. Usually abuse occurs over a long period of time. Once the abuse is discovered, the congregation feels betrayed and foolish for having trusted someone for so long. The abuser may be dismissed even before the majority of the congregation is aware of the evidence, leaving many to mistrust those who handled the problem. The resulting division is complicated by the efforts of some to return things to normal as soon as possible, without giving the church sufficient time to grieve. The next person in this office will likely have a limited term, providing a buffer while the congregation heals.

- Changing financial circumstances and numerical decline may prevent a church from having full-time ordained clergy or may significantly reduce the pastoral staff and the church's outreach. Transition does not always occur in a statistically upward way. Unless the congregation takes time to reflect upon the way it is being reshaped, a spirit of negativism may threaten the church's survival. Instead of focusing on the things lost, the church needs to prayerfully seek new relationships, often inviting other ministries to share its building space or forming a partnership with an adjacent parish.

- A church has a series of short-term pastorates (three years or less) and/or the abrupt and unplanned exit of a pastor. In the past, the fact that ministers did not stay long may have been attributed to bad luck; but now denominational officials are insisting that the church's leaders do an honest self-evaluation. Many churches feel that they have been stuck in this revolving door by economic circumstances because they cannot pay their clergy much. This lowest bidder status means that they always receive those who are just coming into ministry (preparing for ordination) or those who are ill-suited for ministry and are running through pastorates, leaving just ahead of being fired. Given the high cost of moving and preparing for a new pastor, it is hard to make much of a financial case for remaining in this cycle. Making the transition into part-time ministry may provide for greater stability. No matter what the cause of short-term pastorates, the effect is a loss of congregational self-worth. People emotionally close down and become unwilling to share their feelings with their pastor. They feel that something is wrong with their church if none of the last three clergy have loved her enough to stay. A new pastor will not be able to break the cycle and minister to the congregation unless a period of transition and healing shifts this communal sense of guilt into the past.

In each of these situations, the effects of the trauma linger long after an immediate solution is found. If a change in pastoral leadership occurs, the new pastor is likely to be short-term, forming a bridge between the leadership style of what was going on when the crisis occurred and what needs to happen in the future to keep the church stable. The focus of such interim ministries is healing. The congregation needs to give itself time to grieve and to work through the steps that will lead to a healthy transition. The congregation will need to limit what it expects of itself, both in terms of doing new programs and in terms of maintaining former glory.

2. Conflict Inside the Church

Conflict is a frequent visitor to church life. Yet when conflict comes to our congregation we feel isolated and wonder what is wrong with us. At times, a mismanaged interpersonal conflict results in a significant group of people walking away from active church membership. This "losing side" may be only a small percentage of the total church membership, and some of this group may even continue to attend worship. However, a sense of frustration descends on all aspects of the church's life. Outsiders may come to view the church as a "conflicted church," a reputation that sticks long after the original issues are resolved.

The good news is that in most cases the church can move on and find healing. It can discover a fresh sense of confidence and be free to do new forms of ministry. After completing a period of transition, the remaining church members will look back and notice how often opportunities for growth were missed in the past because the church's key players had conflicting visions about what being a church meant. Turf wars and poor avenues of communication can sap a church of energy for a long time before a visible church fight breaks out. Successful negotiation of this stressful time requires looking beyond the blame game, choosing instead to change the way the whole congregation works together.

Engaging in a period of transition provides the needed time for church leadership to learn better relational skills and to think objectively about how they conduct business. Instead of focusing on how certain individuals behave, the transition process invites us to see the entire church as a system. When disagreement breaks out in the future, the congregation will be slower to polarize into opposing factions.

3. Neighborhood Problems

Economic shifts in the community, whether positive or negative, force the church to rethink where it gets its finances and new members. A new expressway may bring a flood of opportunities and/or the sudden need to relocate. As the neighborhood shifts, programs that were once successful may no longer be viable, and members may be left feeling as if the energy of the whole church has "gone south." Churches who fail to honestly face what is happening around them will become stuck and will eventually close. As they say in the real estate business, "Location is everything."

But the church is more than a building stuck on a particular piece of property. It is a living congregation, a dynamic doorway for people to encounter the love of God. The closing of a major employer in a community does not eliminate the need for a church to exist but, rather, shifts its target for ministry. The wise congregation, when faced with a changing neighborhood, becomes willing to risk anything for the opportunity to meet the

The effects of a trauma linger long after a solution to the problem is found.

needs of the current context. They may have to give up a cherished building or open up to a new group of people, but change becomes their ally rather than their enemy.

Intentionally choosing to enter a period of transition enables the church to focus not only on how it will respond but also on who it will be. Having a sense of congregational identity and a shared history becomes a powerful resource for shifting into a new gear and meeting these challenges. The population and cultural changes that occur in the community, while they close off old doors, also surface new areas of human need and create opportunities for aggressive outreach.

Trauma Must Be Dealt With

If your church has suffered one of the traumas mentioned above, there is good news and there is bad news. The good news is that this event has probably led many in the congregation to be more receptive to change. The high levels of anxiety that accompany these traumas create a fish-or-cut-bait atmosphere. Either this tension will get resolved or the church will implode. Trauma is often the best catalyst for healthy discussions about where the church is heading. There may have been years of accommodation to practices that limited the church's growth and decade-long conflicts that quietly drained the church's energy. Trauma stops you in your path and causes everyone to pay attention.

The bad news is that when you are at a dead stop, it is hard to move in a new direction. That is why the first step of transition is called Park. Just as parking a car in a safe location, and perhaps getting it towed to a service station, is the first step toward repairing an automobile that is running badly or is no longer safe to drive, so entering a state of being parked is an appropriate response to trauma in the church. And even though the purpose of a car is not fulfilled if it always remains parked, it is a good place to be for a season of repairs.

For Discussion

1. In what areas of your congregation's life is current reality falling short of your personal expectations?

2. What have been the most traumatic times of change in your personal life? How did you get through those times?

3. Which of the following events is driving your church's current interest in having a period of transition—loss of or betrayal by pastoral leadership, conflict inside the church, or neighborhood problems?

4. Do you feel that the congregation is currently in need of a period of time to grieve and work toward healing? If so, how long a period do you anticipate?

5. Can you describe in ten or fewer words what is currently happening in the neighborhood around your church?

6. In only one or two words, describe your current attitude toward change.

Trauma
is often the
best catalyst
for healthy
discussions
about where
the church is
heading.

12

Chapter 2
How the Bible Talks About Transition

When a caterpillar transitions into a butterfly, it first spins a cocoon and enters a period of being hidden from the external world. There is something mysterious not only in the physical changes that the creature undergoes but also in the mental ones. The caterpillar ceases to think in terms of crawling slowly across a leaf and learns instead the complex language of flight. It no longer thinks in terms of making its living by chewing, but focuses on drinking nectar and finding a mate. The church, too, when it goes through a transitional phase finds itself in need of a period of seclusion and internal focus. A church rarely matches the butterfly in physical change, but often a church has the same degree of mental transformation to accomplish.

The Bible presents a variety of examples of people undergoing periods of transition. In each of the biblical stories of transition, the people are cocooned by something that both protects them and prevents them from exiting their time of transformation prematurely. When Noah's family made the transition from their antediluvian world of sin to our present era, they were secluded in an ark. The most obvious form of this transitional cocoon in the Bible is wilderness, but it can also be seen in the grave that Jesus borrowed, in the whale that Jonah met, and in the upper room in which the disciples waited for Pentecost.

For the church recovering from trauma and working through a period of transformation, these stories take on a special meaning. They give hope that we are not wasting our time as we focus on our process. They help us sense that God is still present with us even though the situation around us looks bleak. By focusing on these stories, both in the congregation's worship and in the devotional life of committee members, the church unites around a common language to express feelings, hopes, and faith in the God who is leading them through a time of change.

Transitional periods have always been a part of God's method for leading people.

The Biblical Pattern

Transitional periods have always been a part of God's method for leading people. The story of the Exodus clearly dramatizes five elements experienced by churches today.

1. Trauma

For nearly four hundred years the children of Israel lived in the land of Goshen. During that time, change occurred gradually. While the people saw the political situation worsening, they were unwilling to act on their own for change. Then a trauma occurred. The pharaoh began ordering the deaths of Hebrew children. The people cried out in prayer. God responded by sending Moses, who caused the Egyptians to treat the Israelites even worse. The trauma intensified; the plagues that afflicted Egypt disrupted the normal programmatic life of the Hebrew community and lead them to fear extinction.

2. Signs of Promise Found in Worship

Just when things were most desperate, God gave the people the Passover ritual. This sacred act, which eventually became the basis for our Communion ritual, prepared the slaves for freedom and taught them the language of hope. As they formalized a yearly ritual for telling the great acts of God, they experienced the mental transformation that freed them from seeing themselves as victims of their circumstances.

3. Entering the Wilderness

As the people passed through the Red Sea waters, they were cut off from all hopes of returning to what they once were. They murmured and complained about how much they missed their past life, but going back had now become sin for them. Most narratives of transition have a deep connection to the symbolism of baptism—our way of affirming that God is in the midst of our trauma and has a plan for our redemption. The Red Sea waters were such a symbol for the Hebrews.

4. Lessons on the Journey

Like the butterfly in the cocoon, the people in the wilderness had to unlearn slavery and learn how to be a nation. The journey reconnected them with their history (see the section "Step II: Reverse") as they carried out of Egypt the bones of Joseph and came to understand that the place they were going was once explored by their forefather Abraham. They also learned that the Promised Land would require their effort to conquer, and that there were barriers and giants (see the section "Step III: Neutral") in the Promised Land. They, for the first time, faced their own limits and weaknesses.

5. Shifts in Power

While in the wilderness, the people received a new set of rules to live by: the Ten Commandments. Moses learned from his father-in-law, Jethro, how to delegate authority to tribal leaders and to empower the laity. At the end of the journey, Moses was replaced by Joshua, who represented a new generation. None of those who remembered the old ways entered the Promised Land (see the section "Step IV: Drive").

Further study of the stories on page 15 will reveal many similar elements.

Our Own Experience

The church that successfully negotiates transition will experience each of the following elements of the biblical narrative, though not always in the same order:

- being awakened by trauma
- finding signs of hope in unexpected places
- being "baptized" in a moment of complete dependence on God
- rediscovering historical connections
- learning new patterns of action
- sacrificing old ways of doing things
- transferring leadership
- thinking in new ways about the future

Worship in Transition

This connectedness and experienced linkage with biblical themes empowers worship to be the compass that guides the congregation through the transition wilderness. Worship for the church undergoing transition is like the keel on a sailboat. Hidden beneath the waves of

Biblical Narratives Involving Periods of Transition

Noah and the Flood (Genesis 6:1–9:17)	Note that the transition period in the ark lasted a full year. Churches need to permit the flood waters of change to settle before they can move forward.
Moses' Exile as a Shepherd (Exodus 2:11–3:10)	This transition period began with Moses' failure as a leader. Rather than dismissing him from service, God allowed this setback to be a learning experience.
The Exodus (Exodus–Deuteronomy)	The length and detail of the Exodus story makes it of particular value to churches in transition.
David's First Exile (1 Samuel 19:11– 2 Samuel 5:5)	The Saul/David conflict initiates this period of transition. Instead of permitting the expected passing of the monarchy to Jonathan, God uses this period to bring about a change in the way Israel is governed. There are many lessons about conflict, leadership, and interpersonal relationships in this rich narrative material.
Jonah in the Whale (Jonah 1:17–3:3)	Jonah's calling to go to Nineveh seems to arise from God's desire to transition people out of isolation and into foreign mission work. Chapter 2 displays the importance of worship in the midst of a transition period.
The Babylonian Exile (Daniel Chapter 1)	Daniel and his companions must make the transition to life in Nebuchadnezzar's court. They must decide which items of their old life are essential to faith and which are now obsolete.
Jesus in the Wilderness (Matthew 4:1-11)	This transition period before Jesus' entry into ministry helps us understand the temptations that may distract the church from her primary task.
Jesus in the Grave (Matthew 27:55–28:10)	The entire Lenten experience and Passion narrative lends itself to speaking about transition. It is a wilderness road of abandonment that closely parallels the Exodus story. The joy of Easter speaks to the church's entry into a new future (the Promised Land) after a long season of transition.
The Disciples Awaiting Pentecost (Acts 1:7-26)	The locked doors of transitional introspection precede the open doors evangelizing the world. Jesus did not permit his disciples to skip this step.
Paul in Arabia (Galatians 1:15-18)	Paul needed three years to transition from his life as a Pharisee to the missionary life and new understandings about freedom in Christ.

conflict there needs to be something deep and heavy providing balance. While the captain at the helm may not think much about the keel as he adjusts the sails to meet the winds of change, it is the counterbalance that enables the boat to use the energy around it.

One pastor, when the church he was serving was facing a major transition, gradually increased the time devoted to intercessory prayer in worship. Instead of having a simple musical response precede the pastoral prayer, he used a prayer hymn and invited people to come to the altar. He instructed the organist to be prepared to play additional soft music as needed, giving the people permission to expand this part of the service to meet their need. Few people noticed that he had cut back on the length of his sermons, but several commented that the worship was now more focused on healing. This subtle change supported the church through a difficult time.

Sometimes change is most disruptive in the area of worship. The church may be launching an additional worship service with a more contemporary style of worship. Or there may be a shifting of traditional worship times to make the church more inviting to new members or a different generation. A church may also have to change its Sunday schedule in order to be yoked with another congregation, and therefore be facing both a change in pastoral leadership and a change in worship time.

As these changes occur, it is important to recognize the positive inertia that worship exerts in the faithful church attender's life. To be reluctant to embrace the new service times or a contemporary style of music does not mean that people are being "old fogies." Rather they are being honest about the emotional stability that they have found in predictability of worship. If a transition is going to affect the time or style of worship, then care must be taken to communicate the reasons for this change early and to provide ample opportunity for healthy dialogue. Building consensus one member at a time may be required.

The Appendix (beginning on page 139) provides suggested Scripture texts for use during this time. For congregations who are accustomed to lectionary preaching, adopting these thematic texts becomes a way of marking the period of transition as a distinct time in the life of the congregation.

For Discussion

1. Which Bible stories connect with the experiences of your congregation over the last few months?

2. Read the familiar Twenty-third Psalm. Can you note a set of steps or different stages of life being described?

3. Change can be visualized as falling in one of the following four quadrants:

Change that is positive and sudden	Change that is positive and gradual
Change that is negative and sudden	Change that is negative and gradual

   • Which best describes the changes your church is currently going through?
   • Can you think of a biblical example for each quadrant?

4. How central is worship to the life of your congregation? Be specific about the effect worship has had on the life of people now involved in the church.

5. When was the last major change in the way worship was done in this church? How long did it take people to adjust?

Chapter 3

The Process of Transition

One of the assumptions of this book is that transition is an ongoing process. Even when a church is recovering from trauma and people are not verbalizing any desire to change, there will be change and the need for a period of transition. While we may want with all of our hearts to go back to the way things used to be, change always leads us forward. Transition is to walk intentionally through a series of progressive steps until we can embrace the future as a place where God also is.

Recognizing that there are certain things that must be done goes a long way toward stabilizing a church in trauma. Just as families work through grief following the passing of a loved one by engaging in the tasks needed to have a funeral, so also the church works through a period of upsetting change by doing certain tasks. A church can faithfully work on doing these tasks and come through change successfully, or it can linger in programmatic limbo and die.

Five Developmental Tasks

Loren Mead of the Alban Institute was one of the first to study the relationship between the successful completion of a period of transition and certain tasks that must be performed. In writing about the transition time (often several years long) that occurs between pastors in some denominations, he identified what he called the "Five Developmental Tasks," which he urged interim clergy and pastoral search committees to lead the church to do. These tasks are described below.[1]

Task 1: Coming to Terms With History

It is important during a change in pastors for churches to reclaim both their own congregational history and their denominational heritage. These connections allow current conflict in the church to be seen against a larger backdrop. They also allow newcomers to feel incorporated into what has been cherished and valued by the longtime members of the church.

Task 2: Discovering a New Identity

Church members are often unable to say how their church is unique or special. Today every ministry and volunteer organization needs to be able to identify its own market niche. Just being the church on the corner is not good enough when trauma has created chaos in the congregation. The church has to find a new identity.

Task 3: Allowing Needed Leadership Change

Often when a long-term pastor leaves, the church's power structure shifts as laypeople rethink their personal commitment and roles. The contrasting leadership style of the new pastor may lift to the forefront people whose views were previously ignored. Other people may suddenly find themselves out of the loop. These changes go better if the old guard is recognized for their years of service and if the new changes are instituted in ways that keep everyone informed of what is going on.

Task 4: Renewing Denominational Linkages

The congregation is often unaware of the role denominational structure plays in insuring the local church's survival and health. That relationship becomes more visible, though not always more appreciated, during a pastoral change. One of the tasks of interim ministers and church leaders during transition is to find ways to make the congregation aware of the denomination and the resources it provides.

Task 5: Commitment to New Directions in Ministry

To complete the negotiation of a transition period the congregation needs to shift its attention from the past to the future. A new pastor needs to be recognized for the fresh gifts he or she brings to the task of reaching the congregation's goals. Even if the transition has meant a smaller staff or the loss of a building, the congregation must come to value the ministries that they are now able to perform.

Over the past twenty-five years, Mead's developmental tasks have been widely published and used by many congregations. This book consolidates, reorders, and expands on Mead's description of developmental tasks. These five developmental tasks, as well as many others, are put into a sequential order called The Transition Transmission. Each activity the church leadership completes builds upon the previous one.

The Transition Transmission

The key concept of this book is that critical changes in the local church happen best when they are accommodated within a declared period of transition. A period of transition enables the leaders of the church and the congregation to work together through the steps the congregation needs to experience in order to find healing.

The path laid out in this book is a progression of four steps that unfold through the seasons in the congregation's one- to two-year period of healing. Each season has its own mood and energy level. Each season is supported by close connection with the congregation's experience of the liturgical year in worship. A church may, of course, choose a shorter period of transition. However, the experience will not be as profound as working through seasons in their proper order during at least one full year.

This book organizes the steps of the transition process using the mnemonic device of an automotive gearbox. Just as a person driving a car needs to know how to shift the energy of the engine through the various gears, so the leaders of a local congregation need to shift the energy of the congregation through the various gears of the transition. The gears of The Transition Transmission are Park, Reverse, Neutral, and Drive.

Step 1: Park

Recognize that where you are, as a church, is where you are. God has a purpose for this time and a reason for your being here. Some of the tasks performed during this step are to

- declare a period of transition and define how long it will last;
- identify the conflicts and traumas that mark the church at this moment;
- accept that healing will be the primary task of church leadership for the entire transition period;
- become familiar with group dynamics, recognizing that the church is an interdependent system of groups and personalities and that what affects one committee affects the whole ministry;

- commission small study groups to discover what it means to be a church;
- make definitive passages, such as Matthew 28:18-20 and the early chapters of the Book of Acts, the focal point of congregational worship;
- learn how healthy systems differ from unhealthy ones;
- consider how church committees can do their business more cooperatively.

Step II: Reverse

Come to terms with your history. Celebrate what is good, and examine current events against the backdrop of what God has been doing for the last two millennia or so. Remember that history cannot be changed, but it can be healed. Some of the tasks performed during this step are to

- empower a committee to organize a celebration of your church's history;
- give people an opportunity to comment on various past challenges and achievements of the congregation;
- study biblical stories in which faith enabled the people of God to overcome conflicts and trauma similar to your congregation's traumas;
- construct an accurate church timeline, focusing on statistical information about what has contributed to your church's health and growth in the past;
- lift up relevant connections between your church and the history of your denomination, or the proclaiming of Christ in your region, in worship, and in special programs.

Step III: Neutral

Before the church can transition into a forward mode, the road ahead needs to be checked for obstacles. Some of the tasks performed during this step are to

- survey the congregation to identify areas of weakness or constraint that are limiting the church's growth;
- clearly identify what measurements will be used to assess the church's progress;
- identify what the church may have to lose in order to go forward—selling some facilities, dismissing staff, closing down programs, and so forth.

Step IV: Drive

Now you must choose to do something different, even if it feels wrong. Some of the tasks performed during this step are to

- study the facts that surround the implementation of any change;
- focus on a stewardship program that emphasizes time and talent (or begin other actions to empower people to shift into new leadership roles);
- set policies that will limit the term in office and the influence of people who are fixed upon the prior way of doing things;
- take whatever actions are necessary to overcome the barriers or constraints noted in Step III;
- be willing to take risks and prepare to welcome and recognize failure as a learning experience;
- study biblical passages that emphasize people taking a leap of faith.

Permitting Ourselves to Try

The important thing to note about these steps is how they emphasize the transition period as a time for developing new processes in the church. The congregation needs to come to trust itself again. The church leaders need to know that they can make decisions affecting who they will be in the future. There needs to be permission to make mistakes and to recognize past failures. There also needs to be healing. The local church should also exit the transition period with a restored sense of trust and improved interaction with its denominational leaders.

We might summarize by saying that in transition,

the process is more important than the results.

Note what this phrase means.

- On the level of committees making decisions: It is more important that each person is respected and good discussion occurs around the table than that "the right thing" be accomplished.

- On the level of local church politics: It is more important that changes occur to the structure and the healthy interaction of committees than that "right people" get their way.

- On the level of pastoral leadership: Being a compassionate pastor—spending much more time listening—is more important than preaching or administrating.

- On the level of denominational relationships: The focus is on the church exploring what it means to be a member of this tradition and having a positive experience when it requests help and resources. Only after the church reconnects with its heritage can we expect them to comply with all the directives coming down from above.

- In general: The *way* that we do things is more important than *what* we do.

For Discussion

1. What does the phrase *the process is more important than the results* mean to you? Apply this phrase to something you do, such as teaching someone how to play golf.

2. What happens when the driver of a truck or car misses a gear? Are there other processes where failing to follow steps can lead to less than desirable results?

3. One of the transitional tasks noted above, both by Loren Mead and by this book's Transition Transmission, is coming to terms with history. How well do you know the history of your congregation? (See "Step II: Reverse.")

4. How ready are the people in your congregation to talk positively about the church having a new future? Do you think the steps outlined in this chapter can lead your church in that direction?

Endnote

1 Adapted from *Critical Moment in Ministry: A Change of Pastors*, copyright © 1986, by permission of the Alban Institute, Herndon, VA; pages 36–50. Order from The Alban Institute, 2121 Cooperative Way, Suite 100, Herndon, VA 20171; www.alban.org; phone 800-486-1318 or 703-964-2700.

Chapter 4
Interim Ministers and Other Consultants

Intentional interim ministers are clergy who have been trained to provide short-term pastoral leadership in situations that require healing and additional leadership in the transition process. These pastors work with the congregation for a specific contractual period (often a year) with the clear understanding that they will not be available to serve the church as their regular pastor. These boundaries enable interims to address a church's issues with unusual candor and compassion. They have been trained to enter difficult situations and act as catalysts for change without being consumed by the process.

Denominations that have a congregational "call" system for hiring new clergy often have structures in place to supply ministry during the period when a church is between pastors. Since the mid-1970's, however, there has been growing recognition of the importance of training those who serve these interim situations in developmental tasks such as those enumerated by Loren Mead. This work has led many denominations, whether they have a "call" system of clergy placement or an appointment system, to realize that there are congregations in need of special attention during a change in clergy. Regardless of how a judicatory places a new pastor in a situation, there are some churches who urgently need a buffer period to adjust to the change.

On page 22 is a checklist of factors that may identify a congregation that needs additional help as they travel through this transition period. Ideally, this help would come from a trained interim minister hired to serve the congregation for a one- to two-year period until their regular "installed" clergy could be received. But if such interim pastoral leadership is not available, the congregation might keep on track with their transition if a suitably trained consultant works with their committee on pastor/staff-parish relations and the new pastor. However, the more strongly any of the factors in the checklist are indicated, the more urgently the congregation needs a trained, designated interim pastor.

Using the checklist requires 30 to 45 minutes. The exercise may be done by any size group or by individual leaders. The checklist is particularly designed for denominational officials and consultants meeting with a local church's committee on pastor/staff-parish relations.

> Interim ministers have been trained to enter difficult situations and act as catalysts for change without being consumed by the process.

Congregational Trauma Self-Test

I. Checklist of Risk Factors

Check as many as apply to your church. Underline phrases that apply most specifically to your church.

❑ Your pastor has died or become unexpectedly disabled while serving this congregation. (Note if the congregation feels guilty, as with a stress-related disability, a suicide attempt, or some other circumstance.)

❑ The exiting clergy has served for longer than eight years and/or has made his or her ministry "hard to follow." Check any of these that apply.
  ____ The pastor was controlling or failed to empower the laity.
  ____ The pastor was the founding pastor, or the leader during a change of location.
  ____ The pastor plans to remain in the community and/or displays reluctance to turn the pastoral relationship over to the next pastor.

❑ There has been sexual or financial misconduct by a pastor or a significant church leader.

❑ The congregation's perception of the pastor's character is flawed. (The pastor has become separated or divorced or has sought treatment for an addiction or a mental health condition.) Note if
  ____ there has been a public scandal;
  ____ criminal charges have been presented.

❑ A conflict has resulted in the walkout of a significant group of people from active church membership. Note if
  ____ the resulting financial loss has changed the status of the clergy the church is able receive.

❑ Fire or other unforeseen disaster has resulted in the loss of the church building, parsonage, or a significant mission program. (Check this one even if it has been several years since the event.)

❑ The congregation has failed to complete an approved building project, is in arrears on a mortgage, or has otherwise failed to meet a significant goal that they have committed themselves to.

❑ Economic shifts in the community have forced the church to downsize its ministry or outreach. Note if
  ____ poor stewardship or a poverty mentality has further depleted the church's resources.

❑ The congregation is being forced to relocate for some reason other than growth requiring larger space or the availability of a more desirable location.

❑ The congregation's failure to adjust its ministries to the population or to cultural changes around them is endangering the survival of the church.

❑ The congregation has had a series of short-term pastorates, or the most recent clergy left unexpectedly. (Check this one only if there is now some interest in the congregation to get out of this cycle.)

❑ The congregation is moving toward some type of merger or closing of a church.

II. Evaluate the Present

Checking any of the above twelve factors indicates that a congregation going through a pastoral change is likely to receive value from a designated transition period with a trained interim minister. The more strongly these factors relate to the congregation's situation, the more likely the next pastor will fail to have a lasting, fulfilling ministry without the buffer zone that interims provide.

Note how traumatic you judge the cumulative effect of the above checked items to be on this congregation's current emotional and spiritual life:

1   2   3   4   5   6   7   8   9   10
(not especially traumatic)   (extremely traumatic)

III. Forecast the Future

The aftereffects of each of the traumas listed above can be long-lasting and subversive. The congregation may be haunted for years, falling short of their potential and being unable to manage their own future. A consultant working with the congregation years down the road may bring these issues to resolution, but help through transition provided nearer to the episode is more likely to be effective.

Note how confident you feel about your congregation resolving their own difficulties.

1   2   3   4   5   6   7   8   9   10
(positive, confident)   (concerned, pessimistic)

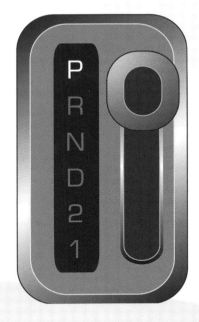

Tasks for Church Leaders in Step I

- Declare a period of transition, defining how long it will last.

- Designate leadership assignments for the transition period, particularly who will serve on the Pilot Group for the transition.

- Provide opportunities for the Pilot Group to grasp the meaning of transitional concepts.

- Tailor the transitional process to contribute to a successful start-up of the new ministry, including acting to prevent a new pastor from being burdened with unrealistic expectations.

- Learn about communication and how healthy organizational systems differ from unhealthy ones.

- Think about how church committees are interconnected and what changes would lead to greater cooperation.

- Commission small-study groups to discover what it means to be a church.

- Make definitive passages, such as Matthew 28:18-20 and the early chapters of the Book of Acts, the focal point of congregational worship.

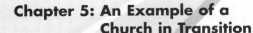

An Example of a Church in Transition

There is a story about someone who randomly went up to pastors at a conference and said, "I'm sorry to hear about the trouble at your church." More than half of the pastors revealed that they were indeed worried about a conflict or difficulty that was rocking their churches. The other half said, "Yes, we were having trouble, but we are through that now."

When trouble comes, our first reaction is, "Why us?" We may have paranoid feelings. We may have concerns that the denomination has labeled us as "a bad church" and that we will never receive a competent pastor again. Clergy experience the same paranoia when they leave a situation in which there has been conflict or a dramatic loss in membership. Yet the truth is, trauma is experienced at some point in the life of every congregation. Unfortunately, what rarely happens is the sensitive use of a transition process to heal the wounds.

The story of Benthair Memorial Church speaks about the roller coaster ride of trauma and transition in the life of a congregation. While this story is fictional, the difficulties encountered are common, and the solutions provided by the application of the transition process display the creativity that is inherent in people who are open to the Holy Spirit.

Trauma at the Crossroads

Benthair Memorial Chapel is a modest United Methodist church at the crossroads. The farmland that once surrounded her is gradually giving way to developments as new highways connect the area with an expanding metro. As the crossroads have become busier, on-street parking near the church has diminished. The church that once primarily served the neighborhood now has few people who walk to it. Many members drive past another United Methodist church on the way to Benthair because of strong family ties in the congregation.

Rev. Max Elder has been at Benthair thirteen fruitful years. While the church has not grown numerically, he can take pride in the church's varied programs. Pastor Max has also been successful in spurring the congregation to participate in mission fundraisers, so that on several occasions they have received honors for being the church that raised the most money in the district to support special mission projects. He has also formed deep friendships in this church and would hate to leave it.

Some, however, would accuse Pastor Max of stacking the church committees with his cronies. He is, in truth, highly energetic and does much of the difficult leadership work himself. He has taken over several jobs that no one seemed to want to do, such as decorating the sanctuary for Christmas. Whenever people complain that he controls things, Pastor Max can immediately point to two committees over which he has no power. As long as anyone can remember, the finances of the church have been the provinces of a small clique. They are always in the background complaining that the pastor's mission projects are a drain on the church. They have fostered the suspicion that the reason the Reverend is so into sending

> Trauma is experienced at some point in the life of every congregation. Unfortunately, what rarely happens is the sensitive use of a transition process to heal the wounds.

25

money to Africa is because it makes him look good to the conference. When several vacancies appeared on the committee on pastor/staff-parish relations, two provincially minded people stepped forward. They soon turned each meeting into an inquisition into how much visitation and "work for us" the pastor was doing. Pastor Max's friends could hear the self-pity in his voice as he referred to these committees as the thorns in his side.

Then the accident occurred. Gloria, who is usually on Pastor Max's shut-in list, had dragged herself to church for Easter. Midway up the side steps, a loose railing gave way, causing her to fall and break her hip. The trustees would have repaired this rail, but the whole staircase was due to be eliminated if the plans for the new narthex building project went forward. Why should they spend money to fix these stairs that were used only by a few old-timers who walked to church? The insurance company was quick to point out that the little yellow "Caution: Loose Railing" sign that Pastor Max had posted only increased the church's legal liability for the accident. "Now we will be wanting some of that mission money back," the finance committee members bellowed.

Soon the district superintendent received several phone calls requesting a change of pastors. She agreed to meet with the committee on pastor/staff-parish relations. That summer several significant church members withdrew from the congregation. Pastor Max wondered if anybody had been listening to his eight-part sermon series on church unity.

As fall began, things seemed to be calming down. The district superintendent urged the committee on pastor/staff-parish relations to fix the problem (that is, settle the lawsuit) and not waste energy blaming one another. This year a sheet describing new guidelines for local church financial accountability was included in the preparation packet for the yearly church conference. Pastor Max told the church council that now was the time to remove the current clique of closely related people on the finance committee and adopt a financial system in line with conference guidelines. The finance committee reacted by questioning if the church council or the pastor had any right to meddle in their affairs.

The new year began with Pastor Max not getting a raise for the second year in a row. What could he expect with the church's current situation? At the church conference, some new members had been added to the finance committee, but no real changes were made to how things were done. In general, participation in all of the church's committee meetings was in decline. New people who agreed to get involved in church leadership frequently complained that most decisions were being made without their input.

On Ash Wednesday, Gloria passed away and her family honored her wishes by requesting a different pastor to do the service. That Sunday some of the trustees met informally in the hallway, discussing if they could afford to place a bid on her house. The timing could not have been worse. Before all this, they had hopes that they might one day be given the property to alleviate their desperate parking situation. Now they had sunk money into repairing a railing on a staircase they did not need, and the insurance company had raised their rates following settlement of the lawsuit. These discussions were soon overshadowed when, at the end of the worship service, Pastor Max announced that he had received an appointment to move to another parish. He tearfully expressed his reluctance to leave, but as he put it, "I must go where the bishop sends me."

Discussion: What Kinds of Trauma Have Occurred?

Before reading the outcome of this situation, discuss these questions.

1. How did Benthair Memorial Chapel experience the following forms of trauma: loss of or betrayal by pastoral leadership, conflict inside the church, neighborhood problems?

2. What negative factors were apparent before the traumatic events of this year occurred?

3. How did Pastor Max's 13-year pastorate help the church? How did it harm the church?

4. Given the events of the past year, how ready do you think the people of Benthair are to trust their denominational leadership to send just the right new pastor?

5. What qualities should the new pastor possess?

6. What details of Benthair's situation resonate with your own situation?

The Next Year

When the district superintendent met with the committee on pastor/staff-parish relations, she found it hard to gather the information she needed. The committee seemed mired in the church's problems. Some found it difficult to think about the future because they were still grieving the fact that Pastor Max was leaving. The conversation kept coming back to the lawsuit and how painful and divisive it had been for the church. There was also an unexpressed tension in the room between those who had supported Pastor Max and those who were his critics. The one expectation they were united in expressing was that the next pastor had to come at a significantly lower salary.

The mood of the entire congregation was like a car stuck in a deep snow drift. The committee on pastor/staff-parish relations hoped that the district superintendent might have a quick answer that would push them out of this predicament. However, Easter came and went without any word about who would fill Pastor Max's shoes. On the first day of May, the district superintendent met with the committee and presented an unusual plan. The conference would not appoint their new pastor in June. Instead the conference would appoint an interim who had been trained in helping congregations work through a period of transition. This Rev. Deacon would serve them for a year. Then they would receive a new pastor who could have a fresh start—and hopefully a long-term pastorate.

Chairperson Bob's response was immediate: "Is the conference doing this just to punish us?" Others expressed a concern that the church would continue to drift and lose members if they did not receive their regular pastor right away. The members seemed to have assumed that given a new pastor, the church could put the whole affair behind them.

It was a long meeting, and the district superintendent went home wondering if she had sufficiently allayed the committee's doubts. She had tried to assure them that having a special pastor to work with them on transition issues was a privilege and that they were lucky to have a gifted interim available and living nearby. She discussed with them the alternative of having a paid consultant work with them and their new pastor. Whatever happened, they needed to work through certain steps to bring healing to the congregation. She had concluded the evening by warning them that unless there was a change in the fundamental systems that underlay the congregation's way of making decisions, the next pastor would have a hard time.

The committee agreed to meet by itself the next week and take the Congregational Trauma Self-Test (page 22) and discuss their own sense of the anxiety level of the congregation. They also began to make a list of those in the congregation who might have had some experience with working through difficult transitions. One of the committee members said that his workplace had recently gone through a major restructuring and that he had appreciated the way an outside consultant had defused some of the workers' resistance to change. Another member shared how a grief support group had helped her make the transition of becoming a widow.

By the end of May, the committee had come to accept that a new pastor was unlikely to dispel all the conflicts and anxiety the church was experiencing. They were now using the term *transition process* to describe the therapeutic work that they and the congregation needed. Not only were they ready to receive an interim, but they were also willing to play a lead role in guiding the congregation through a transition process. While they were anxious to meet this interim, they also wanted to turn some of their attention to having a good farewell party for Pastor Max. The fact that this interim was not their "real pastor" somehow gave them more permission to go all out in saying goodbye to dear old Max.

Rev. Gary Deacon began his interim ministry with a Communion service. In worship, the songs, Scriptures, and message focused on healing. Some noted his promise that during this period of transition, worship would be worship, and that he was more concerned about hearing their personal stories of faith than about telling them what to do or believe. Someone remarked after the service that Rev. Deacon seemed to be the kind of person who would really listen to them.

The day after Rev. Deacon's first sermon, the chairperson of trustees phoned him to tell him that they had decided to put a bid on Gloria's house. He wanted to know if the conference could give them a loan for it. Rev. Deacon noticed on the church calendar that the trustees had not been meeting regularly and asked if he could attend their next monthly meeting before they proceeded with the property. This seemed an odd response to the question, but the chairperson conceded that they would be willing to hold a special meeting after church if Rev. Deacon wished. Rev. Deacon voiced his concern that such a hurried meeting would not do justice to the issue and that he wanted time to get to know them.

When the trustees did meet, the chairman was surprised to discover that the trustees were not unanimously behind him in wanting to buy the house. The interim minister did not say much one way or the other. Rev. Deacon talked about how the committee process was more important than any one decision. He seemed to be concerned that each person present have a chance to weigh in and that a consensus develop before they offered a bid on Gloria's house. Because of an unfilled vacancy there were only eight trustees, and unfortunately they were deadlocked. Unlike Pastor Max, Rev. Deacon refused to cast the deciding vote. He said that he thought the discussion had been helpful and that when they met again next month, he was sure they would have more insight.

What Rev. Deacon did not say to the trustees was that he wanted the finance committee to have an appropriate opportunity to speak to the issue of raising the needed funds for the purchase. His awareness of the former pastor's difficulties with that committee made him even more anxious to build relationships first before seeking particular actions. Like any other visitor to Benthair Memorial, he was aware of the need for parking. He hoped that by the time he left, he would have a committee exploring long-range answers rather than arguing over the ten or so spaces this house would provide. He was also beginning to discover that there were emotional land mines related to Gloria's estate.

At the midsummer church council meeting, Rev. Deacon asked an unusual question: When had the church last celebrated its history? He had noticed the centennial celebration photo in the narthex. Harriet blushed and said that the photo was more than twenty years old. "We sure had fun that day. The bishop came and everything." Clarence calculated that they had just missed their 125th anniversary. "With all that was happening last year, I guess we didn't feel like celebrating." Several joked about doing a 126th anniversary celebration. Then Harriet recalled that old Mae Benthair, the last of the original Benthairs, was celebrating her 90th birthday in October. "Why not put the two celebrations together?" Rev. Deacon remarked. A task force was appointed and everyone left the meeting smiling.

When Rev. Deacon visited Mae Benthair, he found this spry, gentle woman to be a wealth of historical information. He also discovered that she had been best friends with Gloria, and his visit enabled her to get some hurt feelings off her chest. She had appreciated Pastor Max's visits but had always had a sense that he had been obligated to visit her. "He was always such a busy man," she complained. Mae also expressed appreciation for the calls and notes she had received from the committee planning the celebration and said she was willing to help out in any way she could.

Rev. Gary Deacon was unusual in other ways. Since he owned his own home in another community, he was much more like an outsider than a regular pastor. He did not have a personal stake in any of the church's conflicts. His situation caused the trustees to consult with the committee on pastor/staff-parish relations about whether they should be renting the parsonage out while Rev. Deacon was there. No one could remember the last time those two committees had held a joint meeting. While the outcome was the vague decision to rent it only if the right person showed up and could be out in a year, the meeting did have other unforeseen consequences. The committee on pastor/staff-parish relations members spoke of their concern that the parsonage being next to the church and not having a private yard made it less desirable for pastors with families to come to Benthair. The trustees noted that they had been holding money in reserve to fix the roof and the furnace of the parsonage; and besides, they did not like the way Pastor Max's careless yard work had reflected poorly on the church. Then someone suggested that Gloria's house would make an excellent parsonage and the current parsonage would make better parking. Not everyone was ready to adopt this brainstorm, but at least the idea began to percolate in the congregation.

When the district superintendent heard of this, she smiled. If a newly appointed pastor had come up with this idea, it would have been shot down. As it was, the people of Benthair were exploring their own ideas for the first time in many years. One of the qualities she appreciated about Rev. Deacon's ministry was his knack for empowering the laity.

Meanwhile, the chair of the committee on pastor/staff-parish relations also had a discussion with the Sunday school superintendent about the small-group study material they had just used as a committee. Rev. Deacon had encouraged them to study together what Jesus' Great Commission (Matthew 28:19-20) had to say about the mission of the church today. Bob wanted to know if some of the adult Sunday school classes would like to study the Scriptures in relation to the transition process the church was going through.

As the fall progressed, some sparks of controversy and conflict continued, usually involving money issues. While some members of the finance committee obstinately fought the purchase of Gloria's house, they had lacked the votes to defeat the combined efforts of the committee on pastor/staff-parish relations and the trustees. In each of the monthly council meetings, Rev. Deacon had asked for the chance to use the first ten minutes of the meeting to present some short teachings on how to have good communication and productive meetings. Because the members realized that he did not have his own agenda to push, they were willing to accept these insightful lessons.

Behind the scenes, Rev. Deacon did a lot of listening. He not only provided opportunities for people to get hurt feelings off their chests, but he also listened to how they felt about the roles they were playing in the church. He noted those who felt underutilized and sought for ways to fit them into jobs they would enjoy. He was also sensitive to who was feeling burned out and what functions of the church were sapping the energy of those involved. The committee on lay leadership met frequently, and at charge conference most committees received new members. Rev. Deacon worked hard to get church newcomers on the council and on key administrative committees, such as finance. The council even entertained a discussion of having term limits on all church offices.

During the winter, the church entered a special development program that involved taking a survey to discover the church's weakest area and then implementing actions to overcome this barrier to future growth. The results of the survey made the church leadership aware of how isolated Benthair Memorial had become from their own neighborhood. For the first time in over a year, people began to talk about how Benthair was at the crossroads of new opportunities to be in mission right there.

That spring, the council held a goal-setting retreat. The annual fall retreat had been canceled for a number of years due to lack of interest, but this one was well attended.

Some questioned whether they should be setting goals, since the new pastor might have ideas of his own. Bob, however, pointed out that the one thing he had learned over the last year was that the committees of the church were quite capable of making their own plans. He expressed that when the committee on pastor/staff-parish relations met with the new pastor, the committee would like to be able to show him or her the goals and hopes voiced during the retreat. This would help the new pastor hit the ground running, knowing that there were already people in the church committed to active involvement.

One significant decision they did make at the retreat was to engage in an every-member pledge drive in the fall. The finance committee had been asked to do something about stewardship in the past, but it had been years since anything had happened. Rev. Deacon suggested a conference stewardship consultant who could lead them through the process. This process would mean that stewardship would not become the burden of the new pastor. Several volunteers agreed to form a stewardship committee to deflect any criticism away from the new pastor and to act as a liaison with the finance committee.

The announcement that a woman, Rev. Cynthia Largo, was coming to Benthair's pulpit in July was greeted with some surprise. From participating in the history celebration in the fall, Rev. Deacon was aware of both the positive and negative experiences this congregation had had with previous female leadership. He also knew whose feathers were most likely to be ruffled by the announcement, and scheduled visits to allow these people to vent. On several occasions, Rev. Deacon also pointed out how Rev. Largo's gifts matched the church's hopes of evangelizing the growing number of unchurched families nearby.

The committee on pastor/staff-parish relations also began plans for receiving their new pastor. Within two months of her arrival every person in the church would have an opportunity to meet her in a small-group session. When talking with Cynthia about this plan, the committee volunteered to do whatever they could to reduce her other pastoral obligations so that she would have time to make the summer a productive time for building relationships. The newly formed evangelism committee eyed what was going on and wondered if some of the hosts of the home get-togethers would be willing to host neighborhood Bible studies once a month. Cynthia was pleased to see the synchronicity of ideas flowing around the church and was enthusiastic about being their new pastor.

Rev. Deacon's final worship service at Benthair focused on forgiveness and reconciliation. During this service he asked the congregation to forgive him for anything he had done or failed to do during his year with them. He also gave them the opportunity to pray for forgiveness and reconciliation for any actions they may have done to one another. The assurance of forgiveness was sealed with Communion. After the Prayer of Thanksgiving, Rev. Deacon reminded the congregation that in a few weeks they would be breaking bread with their new pastor and he would be celebrating Communion with his new church. The period of transition, like a great circle, was coming to a close. The special learning that needed to happen had happened, and now they would part, each ready to begin again.

For Discussion: Is Healing Possible?

1. What emotional factors led to the congregation feeling "stuck" when Pastor Max announced his leaving Benthair?

2. How receptive would your church be to working with an interim pastor or consultant?

3. What did Rev. Deacon mean when he told the trustees that the committee process was more important than any one decision?

4. How was the appointment of a woman pastor handled? Was it also a transitional issue?

5. What does it mean to be a church at a crossroads?

Chapter 6
How Long Will We Be Here?

hile in Park, we discover the wisdom of the traditional Buddhist saying: "No matter where you go, there you are." It does not matter who did what to bring you to this place; you are here. The focus has to be on the present moment. This is the place we have come to, and this is the church we have become. Instead of immediately trying to solve our problems and hurrying on, we must take a moment to ask ourselves what it is that we like and do not like about the church we have become. Review the list of tasks to be accomplished during the Park step (page 23). Then learn more about how to accomplish these tasks as you work through the rest of Step I.

Declare the Transition Period

As we Park the vehicle of our faith journey, everyone wants to know how long the church will be stuck here. Just as we are often reluctant to give our individual bodies sufficient time to heal when we want to move on with our lives, there is sometimes a resistance in the church toward providing all the time needed to adapt to change. Although there is a great deal of overlap between the transitional steps (Park, Reverse, Neutral, and Drive), each one requires time to be performed. When declaring a period of transition, it is always wise to go for as long a period as circumstances will allow. In the Appendix (beginning on page 139) two timelines are suggested for the standard one-year period for transitions, beginning either in January or in midyear. Suggestions are also made for longer transition periods.

It is important to set the date for the end of the transition period at the beginning of the process to calm the fears of those who may think that the interim minister is a substitute preacher provided because no one else was available. The congregation needs to be assured that receiving an interim period is not a punishment, nor is it the result of no one wanting to serve this church. The period of transition will extend from the public announcement of the appointment of an interim through, and well past, the initial move-in period of the next regular pastor. In fact, an installation service for the new pastor can also celebrate the end of the transition period. The interim minister or consultant, as well as the district superintendent or other denominational officials who have supported the process, should be invited to participate in this service.

A church may also go through a transition period without having a change of pastoral leadership. If this is the case, it is possible to follow the calendar year, using the Lenten period for the study and reflective time of the Park step and then capitalizing on the excitement of Christmas and the beginning of a new year for the celebration of the end of the transition period. The alternative is to begin midyear, during the down time of the summer, with the Park step, then move to the Reverse step in the fall, and the Neutral step

> There is sometimes a resistance in the church toward providing all the time needed to adapt to change.

Having a mission statement for the transition recognizes that the whole congregation is part of a process that has a series of incremental steps.

in early winter. This process gains momentum as it "Drives" towards Pentecost weekend as the concluding celebration.

Once the church council has approved a particular block of time for the transition period, they need to publicly present this decision to the congregation. With bold, clear language the council should communicate the goals of the transition period and the ways it will involve the whole congregation in a learning process. One way to keep these goals before the congregation is with posters and with a banner heading in each bulletin and newsletter, such as the following.

We in the _____ *Church are "Working Through Transition Together."*
June 1, 200x to May 30, 200x

As members and friends, we seek healing,
reconnection with our purpose and faith heritage,
positive structures for making decisions,
and a new vision of our future together.

It is worth having the council devote time in a group discussion to formulate this statement so that the actual wording of the goals for the transition period will fit the circumstances of the church. Thinking about what we hope to achieve in a transition process sets the stage for better communication with the congregation.

Publicly stating that the transition period has a specific duration honors the pain that some members may have felt during the trauma prior to the transition. Those who feel that some mistakes have been made in the past will be informed that it is the intention of the church leaders to engage in a closer examination of what went wrong. All parties are given notice that the transition will be a listening time. The intent, however, is to move on. A limited time period insures that the congregation will not reiterate the past *ad infinitum*.

Having a mission statement for the transition, similar to the example above, recognizes that the whole congregation is part of a process that has a series of incremental steps. Before we can kick the church into overdrive, we must first experience together what it means to be in Park. As the process shifts into Reverse, then later through the other gears, the congregation is challenged to work together and stay in gear. A sense of unity is built around the shared process.

The Transitional Contract

In addition to determining and publicizing the length of the transition period, the church council should write a contract or covenant for this period. This written statement allows all parties to see in black and white the reasons for the transition period, and it lifts up the expectation that dramatic changes will occur in the church. It also informs volunteers and staff that additional duties will be expected during this period. The contract provides common ground for understanding the risks and the benefits of the season ahead. It also requests that all parties pay closer attention to clear communication and be willing to consider new ideas. This contract includes these elements:

- the declared time period for the transition process;
- a mission statement and/or a listing of the goals for the transition (see the exercise at the end of this chapter, page 34);
- the designation of a Pilot Group (see Chapter 8, "Leadership During Transition," beginning on page 39);
- a commitment to meet and study transition, spelling out what groups will need to meet regularly (monthly or weekly) for this purpose;
- a statement of specific leadership tasks such as the expected role of the pastor or any program staff in the transition process;
- elements of any interim or consultant's duties, even though that person will have his or her own formal contract.

Each person in leadership in the congregation needs to approach the transition period as a time when he or she will personally strive to be open-minded about change. Working together will require a willingness to set aside one's own agenda in order to facilitate the flow of ideas. A covenant to work together, such as the following, may be added to the contract:

> *In making this covenant, we express our openness to God's future for the _____ Church. Agreeing to trust our fears and anxieties into God's hands, we will work together to discover a new vision. We anticipate that the church committee structures and the ways we make decisions may change over the next ___ months. We here and now commit ourselves to honesty and open communication. For this time period, working together (having good process) will be more important than obtaining any particular result.*

An Exercise: Making the Transition Purpose Statement

1. What goals do you have for the transition period? For help in this task you may want to look back to Chapter 3, "The Process of Transition," page 17. The following are some possible goals found in Loren Mead's developmental tasks and in this book's transitional steps.

   - Examine the present within the context of the church's whole history.
   - Discover your true identity as a church.
   - Encourage new leaders to become involved in the church.
   - Reconnect with your denomination.
   - Experience healing in your congregation.
   - Reconnect with your purpose for being a church.
   - Come to terms with recent events.
   - Find new ways to make decisions.
   - Improve communication among church leaders.
   - Find a positive vision for the future of your church.

   Your goals may include some or all of these suggestions. If they do, though, be sure to reword the goals to describe their significance in your own congregation.

2. Restate your goals in a simple (twenty-five words or fewer) mission statement for the transition period.

3. Discuss concerns you have about focusing on the transition process for the period designated.

4. Will it be difficult to set aside your concerns for getting particular results at committee meetings to work instead on having a fair committee process?

Chapter 7
Healing Is Incremental

I magine that you have had a serious auto accident. Between the hospital stay and your outpatient rehabilitation, you have been out of action for months. Now you need to take a big final step. You need to get behind the wheel again and drive. You were traumatized by the accident, and some deep ambivalence rules your being. You want to get back to life and return to work, but fear keeps your foot off that gas pedal. For several days you just go out into the garage and sit in your new parked car, learning to breathe . . . in and out, calming your fears. Then a friend goes with you as you slowly move out of the driveway and around the block. A week goes by, and your excursions get longer and more challenging. The day comes when you drive by the site of your accident and find that you are not gripping the steering wheel with panic. That afternoon you call your boss and say, "I'm ready to come back."

Being in transition is like learning to drive again after an accident. You will need the psychological space that just sitting in Park in the garage provides. The normal changes that take place in a congregation are like the feeling that you have when you give up your old car and have to adjust to the layout of the new vehicle's dashboard. The excitement of the new overcomes the natural anxiety associated with change. But when there has been a radical change in direction, or there has been serious conflict, or a traumatic betrayal of the congregation's trust in its leadership, the gut level experience of the active layperson is more akin to the situation of a serious accident as described above.

Sitting in a parked car in a garage may feel silly. Taking the baby steps of transition may irk the congregational and denominational leaders who are anxious to "get this thing behind us." The goal of being in Park is to recognize that where you are, as a church, is where you are. God has a reason for your being here. Jesus spent much of his initial ministry doing acts of healing—before taking on his real work on the cross. He recognized that the congregation of Israel was hurting. His deliberately slow start enabled him to establish a relationship with the people he came to save.

> The goal of being in Park is to recognize that where you are, as a church, is where you are. God has a reason for your being here.

Rehabilitation and Park

While in Park, a congregation begins the difficult work of rebuilding the trusting relationships that are necessary for a congregation to function. During this time, plan activities, study groups, and worship messages that focus on healing. Guilt and shame are common emotions for congregations starting transition, and the grace of God needs to be expressed in a variety of ways. These lessons must be learned while the church is in Park:

- The church still belongs to God and is primarily a place of healing.
- Conflict is part of all human systems and not the fault of certain individuals.
- The trauma experienced by this church is not unusual, nor is it a punishment from God.

35

- While Christians may disagree on how to go about the work of the church, we all belong to God's kingdom and want to see the church fulfill her mission.

- In the midst of change, God remains the same.

- How we work together in making decisions is often more important than what we decide.

Notice how many of the above lessons are the same lessons that a person would have to learn and remember if he or she were recovering from a serious accident. In the weeks that follow a personal trauma, individuals often fight the blame game: "If only I had not taken the freeway, I would have been okay," or, "So-and-so is responsible for my accident." Church members also, following any type of trauma, focus on *what if*'s and who is to blame. These irrational thoughts channel energy away from the process of healing. Churches in conflict find it hard to believe that they have not been singled out for punishment—if not by God then at least by the denominational officials. There is a critical need in this early recovery period to rediscover the faithfulness of God. No matter what we are going through, we are not alone.

Good Conflict

As healing begins to happen in a church, conflict does not go away; it only shifts to where it needs to be. For many of us this is bad news; we find conflict painful. Conflict is like physical pain in that it serves a particular purpose in the body. It can spark us to action as nothing else will. It can also cause us to delve more deeply into healing and self-improvement. Pain and conflict are one of the ways we know as individuals that we are alive, and as a church that we are entering new spiritual territory.

Conflict also serves to refocus our attention on our purpose for being the church. In the midst of conflict we wake up to priorities and sharpen our own sense of what we believe. Further, we learn a difficult but important lesson about human nature and the triumphing power of God's love while we are under the tutelage of conflict.

When Paul and Barnabas entered into conflict over allowing John Mark to accompany them, their shared vision of sharing the gospel was the backdrop to all of their discussions (Acts 15:36-39). If they had not both been passionate about effectively serving the mission field, the dispute would have never arisen. They each saw different aspects of the same goal. They each wanted to make new disciples for Christ and build up the fledgling churches of Asia Minor and Greece, but they were in conflict over procedures and means for reaching that goal. Paul valued a dependability in his coworkers, and Barnabas saw the value of recruiting the next generation for the work.

Like many current conflicts in the church, they were both right. In the end, the parting of their ways allowed more area to be covered for the gospel. Paul must have taken some of Barnabas's insights to heart, because he later recruited the young Timothy. Often conflict stirs the church to greater awareness and action. Paul, in a different situation, writes:

> Some proclaim Christ from envy and rivalry . . . intending to increase my suffering in my imprisonment. What does it matter? Just this, that Christ is proclaimed in every way, whether out of false motives or true; and in that I rejoice.
>
> (Philippians 1:15-18)

What happened to Paul and Barnabas is something we all fear in our own congregation. We will sometimes do anything to keep people from leaving. The Holy Spirit, however, still uses conflict to broaden the work of God's kingdom. Sometimes that happens by people forming new ministries and finding other areas of service within the church, and sometimes we just need to lovingly let people go. It is important that the church not leave the transition period afraid of conflict.

Conflict serves a particular purpose in the body. . . . It is important that the church not leave the transition period afraid of conflict.

For Discussion: Healing Requires Work

1. Rate your willingness, as an individual, to live with conflict. On a number scale from one to ten, with ten being the most willing to accept conflict, what number are you?

2. Have you ever had a serious trauma from which you needed time to recover? Such trauma may include events that were emotionally upsetting, such as the loss of a job or a loved one. What things did you learn during that experience that might apply to the church's current situation?

3. What do people mean when they say, "Time heals all things"? Is this saying always true? What qualifiers would you add?

4. Name the people you know who have left the church due to conflict in the last two years.
   • How would things be different if they had stayed?
   • Is the church now ready to move on without them?
   • What do you feel should be done right now?

5. How aware do you think the current church leaders are of the fact that your church belongs to God? Is there a willingness to trust the Holy Spirit, even if it leads to conflict?

Chapter 8
Leadership During Transition

One of the marks of a church in the first half of a transition process is a distinct lack of joy and congregational energy. Following a trauma, the fellowship needs to learn how to laugh again. During this period, people look for leaders who are capable of contributing energy and unconditional love to the congregational setting. People may have invested a lot of energy into attending meetings and peacemaking (or gossiping) during the trauma. Now they just need to rest.

For most churches undergoing transition, the source for energy has to come from outside of the congregation. If there has been a pastoral change, the new pastor should be aware that this is not the way the congregation is all the time. Interim clergy are aware that contributing energy to the system is part of the job. Often congregations in transition may wish to engage musical performers and plan special entertainment events.

Understanding this need for energy should guide all who are involved in preparations for worship. A transition period is not the time to slack off on the quality of the Sunday morning experience. Worship during this period does not need to be complicated, but it needs to be fulfilling, releasing the emotional tension that accompanies difficult times in a fellowship.

The Pilot Group

Implementing the transition process will require the efforts of a group of leaders who are acquainted with all the resources offered by this book. The term *Pilot Group* plays on both the noun and verb uses of the word *pilot*. The group serves as a pilot (noun), like an airplane pilot, who steers the whole congregation and provides navigational insight to the church council. The group also pilots (verb) by being the first group to test new ideas and to work through the discussion questions that will be studied by other groups in the congregation.

If there is an interim minister or consultant, he or she will be an important member of the Pilot Group but not its chairperson. This group is often the committee on pastor/staff-parish relations. It may also be the church council or an *ad hoc* committee formed of the key leaders of the church and other people who have had life experiences pertinent to organizational change. Often therapists, educators, and business leaders will be familiar with how change was gracefully guided in their field.

Whoever is piloting the process, though, it is important that transitional issues receive significant attention at each meeting of the church council. If the Pilot Group is one of the working committees of the church, then all participants must be committed to scheduling the additional meetings this task requires. If the Pilot Group is a specially created task force, its membership must include the key voices that make or break the success of programs in the church. The Pilot Group must also have sufficient clout in the church structure to keep transitional issues constantly in the foreground of all church business. The task of the Pilot Group is to first grasp the meaning of transitional concepts then diffuse these ideas to the whole congregation.

There will come a time toward the middle of the transition process (in "Step III: Neutral") when some will assume that the church has had sufficient healing. However, in both secular and Christian organizations, change initiatives fail when leaders are allowed to return to old habits too quickly. It is the duty of the Pilot Group to work against this tendency and to remind the other leadership of the church that no one is free to go about business as usual as long as the transition period is in effect.

The Pilot Group sets the cadence for the transition process. They read the material and decide which components need to be brought to the attention of which committees and leaders in the church. They also track the congregation's progress, sensing when another step in transition is ready to be launched. The concept of having a Pilot Group is borrowed from business, in which a small team within an organization is given the task of mapping out what, where, and how the business as a whole has to change. They experiment with new ways of doing things and are given the time to creatively think outside the box. They are guided by the maxim, If we keep doing the same things, we will keep getting the same results. If we want different results, then what must we do differently?

This attitude is important for the Pilot Group even if the majority of the church's members blame the current situation on some event that was outside of the current leadership's control. If the church is reeling from abuse committed by a former pastor, then the Pilot Group needs to discuss how the church can be less vulnerable in the future while still having the kind of trust that supports the pastoral office. The Pilot Group will need to wrestle seriously with how a healthy interaction between laity and clergy looks different from a co-dependent relationship. This level of mature conversation may be beyond the scope of the rank-and-file membership, but some small group in the church has to think through these issues.

Leadership From the Bottom Up

To be successful, the study and the work of transition needs to occur at the grass roots level. Small groups, lesser committees, and people who previously may have been involved in only minor tasks will be called on to carry out the various components of the transition process. Just as the elderly Mrs. Benthair found herself contributing to her congregation's coming to terms with history (see Chapter 5), so will effectively working this process involve everyone. Committee chairs need to be aware that being in a period of transition will create new duties and responsibilities in their areas. The trustees, for instance, instead of concerning themselves only with maintenance issues, will find themselves drawn into reflection on how the church facilities limit or enhance the program life of the church. They may be required to do usage studies and think about long-term trends. The transition process will also require them to listen to what those who use the different parts of the building have to say about it. Interaction among all of the committee leaders of the church should increase during the transition.

When CEO Jack Welch sought to bring about innovative change at General Electric, he fostered a concept called the "boundary-less organization." This phrase emphasized that all people in the business should be free to communicate with others up and down the corporate ladder without regard to status or chain of command. If someone on the production line had an idea that would improve the product, he or she should encounter no boundaries in communicating the idea with those in management. During the period of transition, the church needs to experiment with being a boundary-less organization.[1]

The task of the Pilot Group is to first grasp the meaning of transitional concepts then diffuse these ideas to the whole congregation.

The Three Values

This boundary-less quality connects with a number of values that must be carefully cultivated during any type of transition period.

The Value of Listening: When healing is needed in a congregation, everyone in church leadership must devote more of their attention to listening and less to giving answers. Insight into what has happened and where the church needs to go tends to percolate up from the bottom rather than being established by fiat from above.

The Value of the Outsider: When conflict or other trauma afflicts the church, the people involved in leadership get sucked into problem solving. This vortex of anxiety soon erases perspective, and they become unable to look at the church's situation objectively. Wise leaders during transition come to appreciate the fresh perspective that newcomers and outsiders provide. Committee chairs must be constantly aware of this fact.

The Value of Innovation: When things are running smoothly, creativity is a luxury. When church leaders are overwhelmed by more problems than they can solve, seeking those who can innovate new solutions becomes a priority. The general rule is, the more creatively a person thinks, the less likely he or she is to be currently managing a problem situation. Taking the time to consult with those who are not presently involved with the dilemma increases the odds of hearing a helpful new idea.

Short-term Study Groups

One of the important branches of grass-roots organization in the church is the small group that is given a transitional concept to study. Each of the itemized lists and discussion question lists throughout this book, particularly those on pages 56, 76, 106, and 114, can be farmed out to some group in the church for reflection. Sunday school classes might be invited to devote one lesson a month to discussing one of the book's chapters. Chapters 11 and 12, at the end of this section, are about rediscovering the purpose of the church. These chapters are ideal for joint study by all the groups of the church and are a critical place to get wide-ranging discussions. Study groups may also be initiated specifically for looking at transitional concepts and the biblical narratives that support them.

For Discussion: Is Our Leadership Flexible?

1. Rate from 1 to 10, with ten being the highest, how well your actions show that you positively value each of the following:

   _____ The Value of Listening: Are you willing to listen to others express their opinions? Do you seek to know how those who are less vocal feel about an issue?

   _____ The Value of the Outsider: Are you willing to seek advice from someone outside of the situation for solving a problem in the church? Are you willing to make use of experts and resources from the denominational office?

   _____ The Value of Innovation: Do you value creativity in yourself and in others when you are seeking to solve a problem?

   Have group members rank themselves individually on these values. Then ask them to think in terms of how they work together as a group and share that ranking. Invite them to discuss their rankings.

2. How would you rate the current energy level of the congregation? (Check as many as apply.)

____ high; ready to try new things

____ sparking; high energy, but a lot of people are getting burned out

____ plenty of energy going in the wrong direction

____ medium; not unusual

____ temporary shutdown; power is off for repairs

____ losing energy

____ totally out of steam

3. What is the enthusiasm level of your key leaders or pastor? Is it different from that of the congregation?

4. What kind of things would contribute positive energy to the congregation?

5. Is there much laughter or good humor in the church? How does this relate to the energy present in the church?

Endnote

1 See *Jack: Straight From the Gut*, by Jack Welch with John A. Byrne (Warner Books, 2001).

Chapter 9
Leadership Interdependence (Systems Theory)

One of the marks of any church in transition is a generalized feeling of anxiety. The slightest occurrence seems to set off rumors and allegations. There are tempests in every teapot. Committees within the church may still have civil meetings, but participants go home feeling as if they have spent the evening walking on eggshells. Will things ever get back to normal? Why is effective communication suddenly so difficult?

Imagine the church as a mobile. Each element of this dangling sculpture is connected and related to another. In the church, not only do the actions of individual members upset and influence the response of others, but each committee also dances in balance with or reaction to other groups in the church. When the church is in a state of high anxiety, it is like a mobile that has received a push and now is uncontrollably oscillating and gyrating. Merely making one piece stable will not improve the way the whole system is behaving.

Moving beyond this analogy, transition in the church allows for discussion through which the way various elements of a system are interrelating can be changed. For example, before the transition period the people involved in leading the church's contemporary worship service may have had to seek approval for various aspects of their service from the church worship committee, whose members, by and large, were not sympathetic toward this "newfangled" service. The anxiety generated by this conflict spilled out into other relationships in the church. The pastor was constantly being drawn in to take sides, and her total ministry was jeopardized by her sympathy with several of the people involved. After the transition, not only did the contemporary worship team receive a more independent place in the church structure for reporting their concerns, but the fears and suspicions that fueled this enmity were brought into an open discussion as the church thought about its mission and hopes for the future. In taking a total systemic approach to the problem, the anxiety level of the whole church was brought down a notch.

Mapping Linkages: An Exercise

(*This group exercise will require an hour and a half.*)

- Draw on a large, portable dry-erase board a rough draft of the structure of your church, as if it were a mobile. (It is okay to limit the scope of this project to the major individuals and committees. See example on page 44.)
- Cut circles of construction paper and label them to identify each major group and program in your church.
- Cut and label small triangles to represent the committee chairs or other influential individuals who are associated with these groups.
- Place the circles and triangles in the appropriate places on the diagram. Remember that some leaders, such as the pastor, may show up as triangles in several places. The goal is

> In the church, not only do the actions of individual members upset and influence the response of others, but each committee also dances in balance with or reaction to other groups in the church.

to assemble on the board a two-dimensional representation of the church's interdependent system. Keep in mind that the church is actually like a three-dimensional mobile, with each piece influencing the stability of the whole through its links and connections.

- Now think about who influences whom in the decision-making process of your church so that you can assemble the mobile to show the actual relationships between the various groups and individuals in the church. Be careful to illustrate the way the various groups and individuals *actually* interact rather than how they are *supposed* to be related. If you have trouble placing one of the committees or groups, ask if that committee or group is still actively influencing the church, or if it is now present only on paper.

- Using a colored marker, draw vertical lines (representing the strings of a mobile) to indicate how each group is accountable to another group or person.

- Draw horizontal lines (representing the rods of a mobile) to link together groups that influence each other, or perhaps compete with each other for the same resources. Most groups find this linking activity a far more difficult and frustrating exercise than they would have expected. One of the lessons to be learned, though, is how complex and interrelated even the smallest church organization is.

- Now go back to your illustration on the board. Use a marker of a second color to change the connector lines to represent the nature of the relationships the groups have. Do groups have a history of missed communications or conflict? Do individuals refuse to work together? Use the following types of lines to draw each relationship:

  ————— Normal Line: Indicates an honest, functioning relationship

  ═════ Double Line: Indicates a relationship that is enmeshed; that is, the relationship is so close that one of the groups can no longer think or act on its own. Use this line in your church diagram to show when an individual dominates a committee or when one group is often overruled by another one.

  —/ /— Broken Line: Indicates a relationship that is broken so that neither group recognizes the other.

  ⋀⋁⋀⋁⋀⋁ Jagged Line: Indicates a relationship that is conflicted or has been characterized by poor communication.

  - - - - - - Dashed Line: Indicates influence that is hidden. Only a person who has been around a while may know that this person or committee controls that program.

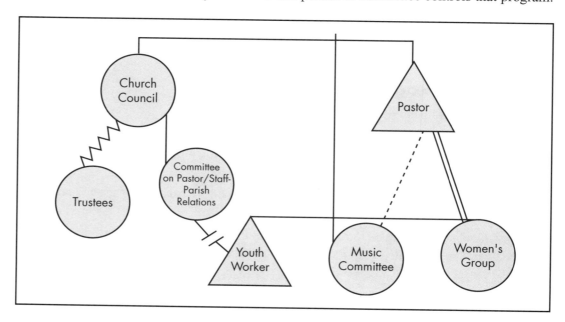

Step back and ponder your completed diagram.

- Notice that most lines are normal. When someone says that the church is conflicted, they are not saying that the whole system lacks the ability to communicate, but rather that broken and conflicted linkages are generating a stress that is felt by the whole system.

- Where in the diagram should the transitional group focus their efforts for improving communication?

- Were any surprises revealed by doing this exercise?

- Remembering that conflict is not always bad (see page 36), note that jagged and broken lines are most likely to impair the long term work of the church.

Store your mobile so that it can be referred to or changed throughout the transition process. Note: You may want to make a small, simple, three-dimensional mobile with string and rods as a visual illustration of the dynamic nature of church relationships. You can display this symbol at church council meetings.

Sharing Responsibility and Authority

The church, like any organization, needs to assign to various committees and individuals the responsibility for making decisions and overseeing tasks and programs. New committee members will often ask, "What are our responsibilities?" Sometimes this question can be answered by referring to a printed document that lists job descriptions for what each committee will do and keep track of. More often these responsibilities are vaguely defined and open-ended. The agenda of each meeting is built around things that we have attended to in the past and whatever new ideas seem to fall into the committee's bailiwick.

In a healthy organization these responsibilities correlate well with the authority and the trust that the whole organization has placed on the committee. When the church establishes a committee, it says, "You are responsible for x and y and z," and also says, "You are given the authority to decide these matters and to spend the money in this budget line." When a church is dysfunctional, however, people are given responsibilities but denied authority. They may feel called, trained, and passionate about a task but frustrated by the unwillingness of others to let them implement their decisions. This leads to rapid turnover and reinforces the reluctance of newcomers to serve in leadership roles in the church. Consider these examples:

- A Sunday school superintendent might be given the responsibility for seeing that every class has a teacher, but is not trusted with the authority to recruit and train new teachers.

- The worship committee meets regularly, feeling that they are responsible for worship; but all of their decisions are ignored by the pastor, who takes total control of each service.

- A new committee is appointed to address some felt need but is not given the authority to spend any funds from the church budget.

- A trustee chairperson makes many decisions without consulting his committee. He justifies these actions by saying, "They are all so busy that I didn't want to call a special meeting."

- Another trustee committee severely limits the youth group's activities and meeting places. Having to get permission for everything was a shock to the couple who volunteered to lead the group.

- A task force is formed with the implication that the results of their study will be considered at an upcoming board meeting, but their report is never given much attention. The task force members are left wondering why they were asked to study the issue.

When a church is dysfunctional, people are given responsibilities but denied authority.

Sometimes what creates this divorce between responsibility and authority is a lack of trust. In the case of the youth group leaders above, a careless incident involving previous youth leadership may haunt their current relationship with the trustees. Until this lack of trust is openly identified and discussed, neither side will fully meet the expectations of the other.

There are many people who rise to positions of leadership in our society without ever learning how to share responsibilities or delegate decisions. The pastor who refuses to share worship planning responsibilities with the laity may justify this attitude as necessary to preserve the authority of the pastoral office. However, effective leadership is defined by the capacity to delegate and to cultivate the skills of those with whom one can share both responsibility and authority. When we do this, we draw more and more people into fulfilling paths of service. In fact, as we will see in the final chapter of this section, the purpose of the church involves recruitment, training, and the sharing of power. We call this "making disciples."

Often the individuals and committees who currently wield power are reluctant to envision the church as a dynamic, changing system built on relationships of trust. For them, the church is a hierarchical pyramid, and authority flows from the top down. Little in Jesus' teachings, or what we know of the early church, supports this rigid structure. Today few people want to become involved or volunteer in an organization that lacks flexibility.

Looking at the mobile of your church system, you may note how some controlling individuals extend the dashed lines of hidden influence while keeping subordinates subject to their authority. Examine each of the vertical lines that is conflicted (jagged /\/\/\ or broken —/ /—) to see if the individual at the top has fully entrusted those below with both sufficient independent authority and meaningful responsibilities.

William Easum puts the matter bluntly, writing:

> The life and spirit of established churches is being drained by mean-spirited people called *Controllers*. Controllers are those leaders who withhold permission or make it difficult for new ministries to start. Control and the abuse of power and authority have no place in the Body of Christ. It is time for us to either convert or neutralize the Controllers.[1]

As a predominantly volunteer organization, the church rarely has formal definitions of how the different offices and committees relate to one another. Most church councils, as they oversee the workings of the church, rarely pause to reflect upon the organizational structure or to ask if they are sufficiently empowering others to feel meaningfully employed in the church. No matter how often we rewrite the church's bylaws, we cannot mandate a spirit of fair play. But the leaders in the church can go on record stating that they will seek to support those who volunteer with the training and authority appropriate to their responsibility. We will return to this issue when we consider shifting the power structure of the church in "Step IV: Drive."

Endnote

1 *Sacred Cows Make Gourmet Burgers: Ministry Anytime, Anywhere, by Anybody*, by William M. Easum (Abingdon Press, 1995); page 31.

Chapter 10
Pastoral Change

When a pastoral change occurs in the midst of a transition, there may be a tendency to focus only on that event. One of the fundamental assumptions of this book is that whatever the immediate events that precede a transition period, the church has larger issues to handle than just who will be the next pastor. Even if the crisis that led the church into transition was some dereliction of duty or serious abuse on the part of the exiting pastor, a congregation who does the healing process well will uncover many latent issues within themselves that need to be discussed. Leadership failure always occurs within a context; and if a church wishes to move into the future, its members must have the courage to examine all of their expectations and vulnerabilities in regard to the pastoral office.

The transition process, even when it occurs during a change of pastors, is primarily about the church's own sense of identity. Each new pastor in some way contributes to the church's growth and development, but what the church becomes is determined much more by the faithfulness of the people and the context that God calls her to minister in. For most churches, the benefits of working through a successful transition process will play out two and three ministers down the road.

Pastoral relations committees may feel under pressure, both by the congregation and by denominational officials, to move quickly in providing information for the search process. The members of this committee, though, may still be in shock and grief and not yet able to work well with the clergy placement process. Succumbing to this pressure does not help the transition process.

As the transition process progresses through Park and Reverse and toward Drive, the church leaders and the pastoral relationship committees get a better handle on the church's true identity and become better equipped to work with the clergy placement process. The Congregational Trauma Self-Test in Chapter 4 (page 22) is particularly important for the church committee that is being consulted about the next clergy placement.

It is also important that local church leaders become students of the particular clergy placement process that will provide their next pastor. Even within the same denomination, different synods or conferences have different procedures and tools for placing clergy. To have the attitude that "the whole thing is out of our hands; the bishop (or whoever) will just send us whoever he or she wants to send us" is to misunderstand the nature of denominational structures and to set the congregation up for discouragement. Those churches who are clear about what they want get their needs met more often than others, no matter what the clergy placement system. Much like life in general, the more we act as if we have the freedom to choose, the more often our choices make a difference.

> The transition process, even when it occurs during a change of pastors, is primarily about the church's own sense of identity.

One pastor tells the story of being hired to serve a small student church.

> I preached my first sermon and thought I did okay. Everyone looked pleased to have me. There was a board meeting following the service to approve my salary. It began with the board chair reporting that "Dr. Cook says this is the last student pastor he is sending for us to try out and we had best accept this one." I felt some of the wind let out of my sails when I was passed by only a narrow margin.

Publicly stating such low expectations for the new ministry sets up both the congregation and the pastor for disappointment. The pastor above later reported encountering difficulty when he proposed a new program in the church. One of the members challenged him, saying, "The seminary sends us a new pastor every year or two. All of them want to change us, and we just wait them out."

The failure here is not with the clergy placement system, nor with the congregation's intransigence, but rather with both parties' failure to work intentionally with the process. When church leaders feel as if they have done the best they can in making the system work for them, they feel a greater confidence in their new pastor. When denominational leaders ask the right questions and get clear answers, they feel more confident about the pastors they place. Both sides of this process are benefitted by a church working through a declared transition period.

It is important when a new pastor is introduced to a congregation that there is a positive reception. Energy is needed to build acceptance and support for both the person and the changes he or she will bring to the church. Energy is often in short supply in churches beginning a transition period. The committee in charge of pastoral relations needs to thoughtfully plan the reception celebration and the pastor's introduction to the various groups in the church. The goal is not only to make the pastor and his or her family feel welcomed but also to publicly state the church's full acceptance of the pastoral authority.

Former Pastors Who Hang On, and On, and On

A country-western song by Dan Hicks asks the question, "How can I miss you when you won't go away?" Congregations are often unaware of their own need for closure at the end of a ministry. Pastoral ministry is, by its nature, relational. To be successful, a pastor not only has to preach well but also has to love well. Relationships are sometimes businesslike and task-oriented as the pastor leads the work of the church committees. They are sometimes compassionate and tender as the pastor provides comfort to those in need. Every pastor also forms with varying intensity relationships of friendship that serve the mutual needs of the pastor, the pastor's family, and the people they call friends. These differing forms of relationships are woven together in an intricate pattern throughout the years of a pastor's service to a congregation. Pastors themselves have a hard time distinguishing which relationships fall into each category. But when a pastor leaves the employ of a local church, these threads need to be separated. Both the emotional health of the pastor and the spiritual health of the congregation are compromised when relationships are not adequately closed and a space created for the new pastor.

A pastor may, sometimes inadvertently, leave his or her business relationships with the congregation unfinished by implying that he or she is still available for consultation. The church committees, on the surface, may act as if the new pastor has been fully installed in the leadership role; but the invisible presence of the former pastor's style and wishes exercises real power in every decision brought to the table.

One pastor tells the story of being at a church for three years when the proposal for a building project surfaced. Several of the board members expressed an interest in asking the former pastor, who had retired within the area, what he thought before they voted. For them it seemed reasonable because in their minds this former pastor still had a business relationship with the congregation. For the new pastor, though, this was a serious breach of her authority and revealed that she had not come as far in establishing her own business relationships with the congregation as she would have liked. However the former pastor weighed in on the issue, his influence was still clouding the judgment of the people.

Some former pastors go much further in sabotaging the new pastor's capacity to initiate new programs or exert a different style of leadership. Throughout their ministry they may have entangled the three forms of pastoral relationships by stacking the committees of the church with their friends. Even though they no longer officially serve the church, contact with their friends still involves them in making decisions about the daily operation of the church. This problem may be worsened if the people prejudge the new pastor to be less capable at administrative matters because he or she is younger or of a different race or a woman. Agism, racism, and sexism undermine God's generous distribution of spiritual gifts and graces for ministry and are deadly to any church wanting to move into the future.

The committee handling pastoral relationships should carefully use the farewell service of the exiting pastor to help the congregation understand that their pastoral care has been transferred to their new shepherd. The litany at the service should include statements such as the following:

> **Congregation:**   We express our gratitude for your time among us.
> We ask your forgiveness for our mistakes.
> Your influence on our faith and faithfulness
> will not leave us with your departure.
>
> **Exiting Pastor:**   I accept your gratitude and forgiveness, and I forgive you,
> trusting that our time together and our parting are
> pleasing to God.
> I release you from turning to me and depending on me.
> I encourage your continuing ministry here
> and will pray for you and for your new pastor, *Name.*[1]

The people may not feel ready to turn to the new pastor for compassionate support in times of grief. They may feel justified in asking someone they know well to perform their weddings and baptisms. If a former pastor answers every call to counsel the distraught, bury the dead, and bless sacred events, then he or she is interrupting an emotional transference that the congregation needs to make, as well as endangering the faith development of any new Christians in the flock. Unfortunately, there are pastors who have difficulty releasing this relational thread. They want to be seen as superpastors, somehow irreplaceable.

What is at stake is greater than the feelings of the individual laity or clergy involved. The church must be seen as an ongoing instrument of God that transcends the ministries of individual pastors. Many people in the congregation, especially if they have joined the church under the old pastor, may have a hard time distinguishing their loyalty to the former pastor from their loyalty to the church. Helping people see that the church continues while pastors come and go is a task that every pastor needs to take seriously. This is what the apostle Paul was attempting to do when he wrote to the church at Corinth, saying:

> For when one says, "I belong to Paul," and another, "I belong to Apollos," are you not merely human? What then is Apollos? What is Paul? Servants through whom you came to believe, as the Lord assigned to each. I planted, Apollos watered, but God gave the growth. . . . For we are God's servants, working together; you are God's field, God's building. According to the grace of God given to me, like a skilled master builder I laid a foundation, and someone else is building on it. Each builder must choose with care how to build on it. (1 Corinthians 3:4-6, 9-10)

The church must be seen as an ongoing instrument of God that transcends the ministries of individual pastors.

The incidence of former pastors being asked to do weddings and funerals is a bell-wether of how well a congregation is going through the transition between pastors. The lay leadership of the church can help get this transition back on track by being willing to confront former pastors who abuse their privileges and by verbalizing their commitment to the church that endows each current pastor with sacramental power. The church's own laypeople are able to exert more influence in this area than the denominational authorities or the new pastor.

Finally, it is only natural that clergy and their families will continue to communicate with friends they have made in their former congregation. In the months that follow leaving a parish, a natural winnowing occurs. The pastor finds that while he or she thinks fondly of a great number of people, only a few continue on as friends. This friendship is based upon mutual interests rather than on church concerns. Some pastors have found that they can continue to have a healthy relationship with friends in a former parish if they practice a "don't ask, don't tell" policy. They never ask about what is happening in the church, and they never tell what they think about what the new pastor is doing.

Clergy Burnout

It is important for churches to realize that the new pastor and the pastor's family are going through a state of transition themselves when they arrive at the church. This transition may involve personal factors, such as becoming more or less distant from their families. It may be highly symbolic, such as moving into the parsonage as new empty nesters and for the first time having bedrooms that do not belong to the children. The actual availability to come to this church may have been precipitated by a health issue or a career change within the pastor's family. All of these factors carry emotional energy that needs to be discharged through a transition process similar in many ways to the one outlined in this book. The process for individuals going through transition involves

- coming to terms with their own identity (Park)
- reflecting on past experiences (Reverse)
- assessing weaknesses and strengths (Neutral)
- shifting into new activities (Drive)
- developing renewed hope for the future and ambitious goals (Overdrive)

People who successfully go through a psychological transition, such as midlife, walk through these steps, though not always in the same order. It is important to note that the first three steps—Park, Reverse, and Neutral—are low-energy stages. Both individuals and congregations feel less enthusiastic, confident, and empowered in the midst of life's challenges when they are in the first half of a transition process. As individuals, and as congregations, we might put on a show or false front of enthusiasm, behaving frenetically; but this behavior is difficult to maintain. It also takes us away from self-awareness and intentionally fulfilling our purpose.

Unfortunately, a pastor who is at a low-energy state in a personal process may arrive to serve a congregation who is in the midst of their own energy crisis. Here again, honesty is important for both parties. Before the new pastor arrives, the Pilot Group of the transition process needs to communicate just where the congregation is in the process. By working together, the new pastor and the Pilot Group can brainstorm ways to support the congregation's need for spiritual energy. The team should make it clear that they do not expect the pastor to run the transition. It is not an additional responsibility that he or she is inheriting. Part of this mutual discussion should be about what activities and pro-

It is important for churches to realize that the new pastor and the pastor's family are going through a state of transition themselves when they arrive at the church.

50

grams should be put on hold to avoid burning out the congregation or the pastor during the transition.

The transitional issues for the pastor may also involve the difference between this church and his or her prior situation. In Chapter 17 the transition study groups will learn how churches differ in their organization, structure, and attitude depending on their size and geographic setting. These differences seriously affect the expectations church members have for their pastor, and the role that the clergy needs to play in order to facilitate the church's program. If a pastor has moved from another category of church, reviewing this material together can be a learning experience for both parties and possibly avert stressful miscommunications. One pastor writes:

> My new church was only one hundred miles from where I had served, and the worshiping attendance was only about fifty people more; yet I often felt as if I had come from a different planet. In my old church the treasurer reported on income and expenses each month to the council, and people had a chance to propose changes and programs midstream. At the new church, setting the annual church budget meant establishing what could and could not be funded for the whole year ahead. I was in for a rude awakening when I submitted for reimbursement what I thought were routine expenditures, only to have the treasurer say that they could not be paid because there was no budget line for them. This was but one of many shocks that frustrated my initial months. I was already in hot water before I discovered that one of my key roles was to formally oversee the other church employees. In my previous church I had been informal with all the employees, treating them not too differently from the volunteers. I felt I was always behind the eight ball in learning the new skill set of being a good manager.

Clergy may also arrive already burned out because of conflict they experienced in the previous church. This does not mean that the pastor performed poorly or is running from mistakes. Often a pastor is like a fuse in an electrical circuit: The system has a short in it somewhere; so to protect the whole, a small component is allowed to burn through. Some churches blow fuses and dismiss pastors every few years, but they never search for the latent issues within themselves that cause such constant turnover. Often clergy themselves have a hard time expressing what it was in the previous church that caused them to feel taken advantage of. Burnout causes people to feel a loss of passion toward their calling. Clergy will sometimes change churches in hopes that the new setting will rekindle that flame.

For Discussion

If there are clergy present for the discussion of these questions, they should remain silent until all laypeople have commented. They are then to limit themselves to short, specific comments that are reflective of their own personal experience. This is not a forum for redressing all wrongs.

1. What policies does your church practice to prevent a former pastor from interfering in a new pastor's ministry? Are there actions your church should be taking now to prevent this from happening in the future?

2. How has the leadership of the church supported the change of pastors in the past?
   - Have you provided for physical change, such as refurbishing the parsonage?
   - Are there policies that protect the new pastor from being overwhelmed by things that need to be done in the first few months?
   - Have installation worship services and get-acquainted meetings been enthusiastically planned?

3. Have you noticed any signs of burnout in the pastors who have served you? How receptive has the congregation been to providing the re-creation and emotional space that pastors need?

4. Is your church at a low, medium, or high state of energy? How does this affect the expectations you have for your clergy?

Endnote

1 From "An Order of Farewell to a Pastor," © 1992 The United Methodist Publishing House; in *The United Methodist Book of Worship*, page 599. Used by permission.

Chapter 11
What Does It Mean to Be a Church?

Your old jalopy breaks down on the interstate for the fifth time this year. You ask yourself, "Why don't I just walk away from this heap of junk?" As you stand waiting for the tow truck, the fact that you like the car's color is no longer sufficient motivation to get it fixed. When the church is stuck, "because old first church has always been on this corner" is no longer sufficient reason for people to continue to give their time, talents, and money to the cause. The motivation has to be more than mere survival.

When a church goes through transition, people begin to ask, "Why should we bother?" The good news is that many longtime church members will continue to be loyal and support (keep alive) a church through chaotic and conflicted times, even though they may want to leave. The bad news is that being unsure about whether the church is fixable is painful, and uncertainty prevents newcomers from joining. The church's self-centered focus on survival lacks sufficient worthwhileness of purpose to attract new people to her fellowship.

Exercise: Features Versus Purpose

Requires 45 minutes to one hour. May be done by any group of up to 15 people. Larger groups should divide into smaller groups.

1. Label one large sheet of paper "Hope to Keep" and one large sheet of paper "Must Do"; or label two columns on a chalkboard.

2. (15 to 20 minutes) Ask everyone to name things they hope will not change about their church in the near future. As the answers spring up like popping corn, quickly jot them down in the "Hope to Keep" column. Answers may include things like

   • I hope we continue to support our missionaries in Uganda.

   • I hope we have at least a dozen youth in confirmation class this year.

   • I hope the choir sings Handel's *Messiah* again this year for Christmas.

   Three Rules:

   • The items must reflect the personal opinion of the individual and therefore must begin with the word *I*. You may assess a 25-cent penalty every time someone says, "We ought to . . ."

   • No one is allowed to comment—either negatively or positively—on any item another person has named. The statements offered may be contradictory.

   • Each person has the opportunity to contribute as many items as he or she wishes.

   The idea is to fill the page with the good things people have appreciated about the church in the past. List every idea, even the ones that are unrealistic or even impossible.

3. Now focus on the second column. Add the words "No matter what changes, the church . . ." above the words "Must Do." Explain that the group must now decide what things from their first list need to be added to this new column to make a short list of things that if the church fails to do, she will no longer be worth keeping alive. Out of the many things that filled the first column, the group must now work together to discover the few that are essential.

Give the group the same amount of time as they had to create the first list (15 to 20 minutes). This time, though, discuss every suggestion. Items may be placed on the board and then voted down or reworded or combined with other suggestions. Remind the group that they are trying to answer the question, What are the things the church must do to fulfill her purpose as an organization?

Encourage the group to narrow the list down to three or fewer items.

4. Now look back over the items left on the "Hope to Keep" list.

- Which of your hopes have an enduring quality; that is, they would be important to keep one hundred years from now?

- Mark with a star the hopes that the group unanimously agrees should matter in the next century.

- If your church is over a century old, you may want to mark with another symbol the hopes that were important to the church's founders.

5. Finally, go back over the "No matter what changes, the church must do" list.

- Does each of these items have support in Scripture?

- Does each one relate to what your denomination expects of you as a local church?

6. Now reflect on your work. The items placed on the "Hope to Keep" sheet are like the features on a car. The features may be the reason why you like a car, but they are not the main purpose for the car. Cars are taken to the shop and fixed or taken to the junkyard and abandoned whenever they fail to perform their purpose. It is essential that a church be clear about its purpose.

The purpose of this exercise is to help the group narrow its understanding of the church's purpose. Once a few items, or better yet one item, can be stated as the core reason for the church's existence, then people from diverse backgrounds can be united around this common denominator. The church leadership can also be more decisive in advocating needed change, because the task is not to preserve in the future everything that people hope for, but rather to do the few things that the church must do.

Discovering the Church's Reason for Existence

One of the tasks of transition is to enable a significant portion of the congregation to reconnect with the church's purpose for being. The exercises in this book are intended to keep the Pilot Group returning to various aspects of the church's purpose in each of the five steps. In this Park section, the focus is on the general purpose of the church. No matter what changes in the world, there is a general purpose that has to be fulfilled in order for an organization to be considered a church. In Reverse, the purpose of today's congregation is viewed against the larger backdrop of the church's history. In Neutral, the focus shifts to look at what is keeping the church from fulfilling her purpose. When a church stops growing, there is always some barrier that has stalled her progress toward becoming herself. In "Step III: Neutral," we will also look at choosing specific evaluation tools that match your sense of purpose. In Drive, the church seeks to further define her own unique purpose and take specific actions to drive in that direction. In Overdrive the focus shifts outward to the community around the church. We will look at tools that will help the church remain faithful to her purpose in the future.

Take a moment to think about other organizations you belong to. How clearly do the members of these organizations understand the group's reason for existing? Check the website of a group such as Kiwanis International (kiwanis.org), The American Heart Association (americanheart.org), or any group that you feel you have a good sense of the purpose of. Is there a mission statement on the website that reveals why the organization exists? Often there is. Keeping a sense of clear purpose before the membership strengthens any group. In fact, an organization rarely reaches beyond the collective vision of its rank and file.

Unlike these other organizations, the church is not free to determine her purpose by simply discussing what we want to do. Churches cannot escape their relationship to the purpose Christ had for the organization when he called her into being. So discovering the church's purpose is not simply a democratic process. We must consult Scripture, looking for the calling that is hidden inside Jesus' teachings. What kind of an organization did the apostles form as they sought to interpret his words? How does your church relate to the purpose of the early church?

The Bible study and exercise that follow are designed for use in any study group in the church. Once the Pilot Group has worked through this exercise, they should seek to involve as many other church groups, Sunday school classes, and committees as possible. During transition, people who have a fresh rediscovery of the church's purpose become the leaven that raises the dough (Matthew 13:33). The goal of this study is not to make everyone agree, but rather to bring as many people as possible into dialogue about what it means to be intentional and purpose-directed as an organization.

This task of rediscovering one's purpose is not the same as goal setting. Many churches draw up a list of goals in an annual meeting. The church leaders may return from a retreat having created a grocery list of things they would like to accomplish. However wonderful these goals may be, a church in transition cannot find the energy to do them until the root question is addressed: Why are we here? These annual listings of church goals are usually focused on answering the *what* and *how* questions of church life. Any three-year-old can tell you that the *why* question needs to be asked first.

The question, Why do we exist? should also be the subject of worship messages throughout the Park period of the church's transition. Groups doing Disciple Bible Study, Bethel, or Kerygma are in a prime position to reflect on this question. The church council may wish to sponsor a mini-retreat on this theme, as well as to reflect on the "for discussion" questions of the Park section. If a retreat or special meeting is planned, take care to include a few new voices by intentionally inviting people who have attended the church for fewer than two years.

While the pastor(s) should be involved in this step, the group should assume that the clergy do not know the answer. The longer a pastor has been serving this church, the safer this assumption is. In church life, we all soon fail to be able to see the forest for the trees. Individual issues tend to block one's perspective of the big purpose of being the church.

The outcome of this reflection time may be an actual statement of, "As the XYZ Church, we exist to . . ." But the point of reexamining one's purpose is not to create some precise, polished statement that everyone can agree with. Instead, this exercise seeks to cultivate an understanding: We have a reason for being. If the pastor(s) and key church leaders have an intuitive grasp of the church's purpose, it will guide the decisions they must make as to what to fix where. Gradually, worship and the whole of church life can be shifted so that it supports the church's primary purpose.

Exercise: The Church Purpose Bible Study

*(Requires 45 minutes, but can be extended to several hours for a retreat
or series of Sunday school classes. May be done by any size group.)*

Opening Thoughts and Prayer

The leader should say something such as, "The church's purpose for being is something that we rediscover; it is not something that we invent. Because each local church is a part of the two-thousand-year-old discipleship process begun by Jesus Christ, we of the current generation cannot make up our own reason for being the church! The Holy Spirit is more than willing to reveal our purpose when we humbly ask. So, let us pause for prayer . . ."

I. Read Matthew 28:16-20.

- Where is this passage, often referred to as the Great Commission, in terms of the total story of Jesus?

- Could it be considered Jesus' final words to his troops before sending them into battle?

- In what other ways can you express the role this passage might have for those who follow Christ?

- What does it mean to fulfill each of the following commands?
  —"Go . . . make disciples."
  —(Make disciples) "of all nations."
  —"baptizing them" (Who is the *them?*)
  —"teaching them to obey" (How do we teach in the church?)

II. Discuss any other passages of Scripture the group or group leader may feel are relevant to establishing Christ's intended purpose for the church. Some suggestions are

- Matthew 16:15-19 (the foundation of the church)

- Matthew 25:31-46 (expected ministries of Christ's people)

- Luke 9:1-6 (Jesus puts his disciples to work.)

- Acts 1:8 (Jesus tells the disciples to witness.)

- Acts 2:41-47 (the activities of the first church)

III. Reflect on Matthew 28:16-20 and other passages discussed, to examine how closely connected the following issues are to fulfilling the purpose Christ had for the church:

- the style, appearance, or location of church buildings;

- the length of the worship service or the music used in it;

- the tasks done by clergy as opposed to the ones performed by laity;

- the relationships churches of different denominations have with each other.

IV. Using just the Scriptures studied in this session, complete the following sentence:

- Jesus wants the church to . . . (*Keep it simple! Fewer than 25 words! Name only things that apply to all churches, everywhere, at any time.*)

V. Turn to denominational statements to see how your faith tradition defines the purpose of the church.

- What things in the Scriptures studied today are discussed in your denomination's understanding of the church? What things are absent?

Note to the Group Leader: Consult a clergy person or a denominational website for help finding this material. Do not overwhelm the group. Present only a few selected sentences for consideration. For example, United Methodists may discuss ¶¶ 201 and 202 (pages 123–124) in *The Book of Discipline*. For the sake of time, the group may wish to comment only on the following excerpts:

> Under the discipline of the Holy Spirit, the church exists for the maintenance of worship, the edification of believers, and the redemption of the world. (¶ 201)

> The function of the local church, under the guidance of the Holy Spirit, is to help people to know Jesus Christ personally and to live their daily lives in light of their relationship with God. (¶ 202)

(From *The Book of Discipline of The United Methodist Church—2000.* Copyright © 2000 by The United Methodist Publishing House. Used by permission.)

VI. Is your group ready to write its own statement of the church's purpose?

- Remember to keep this "work in progress" simple and write only what you feel could be applied to all churches everywhere and in every time.

Chapter 12
More on Purpose Statements

When church purpose statements are well-written, they strengthen the connection between the current congregation and the disciples who first gathered to hear Jesus' Great Commission (Matthew 28:18-20). These statements may be as simple as: "The church exists to bring healing to the world by forming and nurturing disciples for Jesus Christ."

Even a short statement like this one, though, includes words that have accumulated two thousand years of meaning and now have become jargon. When the church uses catch phrases and terms that are specific to her tradition, she isolates herself from the surrounding culture. Worse still, the congregation may become so accustomed to hearing certain words and phrases that they forget what these words mean. Here are several words commonly used in church purpose statements that may be helpful during the transition period.

Church: A local church is a corporate body; that is, it has a life of its own and functions out of the energy and contributions of many people. It is more than just the sum of its current people and their interests. Churches usually have a life span greater than the average person. They quickly develop a history and a sense of identity that transcends the decisions of their current leaders.

Healing: Jesus did not just use healing as a means to get peoples' attention; it was the fundamental aspect of his mission. The words *savior* and *salvation* are derived from the Greek word for healing. As we witness to Jesus, we must involve ourselves in the social aspects of healing a broken world. Each local church must be intentional about the healing it brings to the community that surrounds it.

Forming Disciples: We form disciples by two means: we nurture the children and dependents God has given us, and we tell others about the saving grace that is ours in Christ.

Nurturing Disciples: To be healthy disciples we need the following:
• worship that is in tune with our cultural filters
• guidance in discovering our spiritual gifts and the resources to do our thing
• personal piety and honest study of the Scriptures
• connection by means of stewardship and personal involvement to the church's corporate act of healing the world
• fellowship with other disciples

Jesus Christ: There are many other institutions that form loving fellowships and have a discipleship-like process and/or religious purposes. The Christian church finds its unique identity in its connection to Jesus Christ.

A More Specific Purpose Statement

While most churches can use a general purpose statement, each church should also think about its own local context. What language connects best with your tradition or denominational heritage? A more specific purpose statement can be developed over the course of the transition that reflects the church's own culture, current size, and situation.

Process and Purpose

Effective, specific purpose statements often sound like a process; that is, they start with what exists and then state how, by God's grace, the church will seek to create something new. For example, consider the purpose statement of Willow Creek Community Church in North Barrington, Illinois: "To take irreligious people and form them into fully committed followers of Jesus Christ." This new thing is measurably different from the old. In the Neutral step of the transition process, attention is drawn to those measurements that most closely connect the church's purpose statement. If making disciples is fundamental to achieving our purpose, then how do we measure the number of people who have become disciples as a result of our ministry?

Getting From A to B

In many ways the church is like a car that is moving from point A in the past to point B in the future. The church is never meant to be static. Even though a church may spend a short period in Park, it is always by its nature a form of transportation. Anytime a car moves from A to B, there are four things involved.

First, there is a vision. Someone has a desire to get to point B. The more faithful the church is to the purpose that Jesus has for her, the less misdirected her journey will be.

Second, the car must be available for the journey. We have all had the experience of needing to get somewhere but not being able to find a car that is available to take us there. Just as we cannot jump in the first car we find and drive off, we also cannot assume that just because we have discovered our purpose, the whole church is ready and available to drive there.

Third, there must be a driver. Leaders must understand enough of the congregational process to get all of the components working safely together. The driver for the church is never just the pastor. The quickest way for the transition process to fail is for the church to leave all its organizational tasks on the pastor's shoulders. This book assumes that a fair number in the church will continue to have an interest in systems concepts and organizational learning long after the transition process is complete.

Fourth, there must be sufficient resources, such as fuel, air in the tires, and water in the radiator. Often when a church has a trauma, the first concern is loss of financial resources. But good stewardship and clarity about how resources are used only arrives later, when the church is regaining its health. In the early stages of getting started again, we do not seek for reserves, only for enough to meet current needs. When an auto mechanic examines a stuck car, he is not looking for a full fuel tank. He only checks to see if there is enough gas to get the car started. If the church masters the above three conditions, she will find gas stations on the way to meet her needs.

Effective, specific purpose statements often sound like a process.

For Discussion

1. What words in the purpose statement you developed in Chapter 11 need additional clarification? What jargon or catch phrases frequently used in your church may be confusing to an outsider?

2. How is forming a disciple different from nurturing a disciple?

3. Which of the following things does a person have to do in order to be considered a disciple of Christ?
   - attend worship regularly
   - understand and use his or her spiritual gifts
   - study the Bible
   - pray
   - be a faithful giver
   - have fellowship with other disciples

4. If your church were a car needing to get from point A to point B, which of the following would be the most likely reason for it remaining parked?
   - lack of vision—People are not sure they want to go to point B.
   - not available—The church is already busy doing other things, and no one is available for the work needed to get to point B.
   - lack of leadership—No one knows how to steer the church toward point B.
   - lack of resources—There is not enough money or time or building space to get to point B.

Endnote

1 From Willow Creek Community Church Mission Statement. Used by permission of Willow Creek Association.

Step II
Reverse

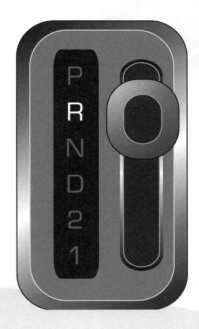

Tasks for Church Leaders in Step II

- Organize a celebration of your church's history.

- Give people an opportunity to comment on various past achievements and challenges of the congregation.

- Study biblical stories in which faith enabled God's people to overcome conflicts and trauma similar to those in your congregation.

- Construct an accurate church timeline, focusing on statistical information about what factors have contributed to your church's health and growth in the past.

- In worship and in special programs, lift up relevant connections between your church and the history of your denomination or the proclaiming of Christ in your region.

Chapter 13
Remembering History as a Healing Act

When God's people were crossing the Jordan River and entering into the Promised Land, Joshua had each of the tribal leaders pick up a stone from the middle of the river (Joshua 4:1-9). These stones were then heaped together as a memorial. This spot was a place of remembrance. Here Egyptian slaves became the free people of God and entered the Promised Land. In placing these stones, they were marking the occasion so that future generations would be reminded of their heritage.

Whenever people pass through difficult transitions, they raise monuments of this sort to give hope to future generations in their struggles. The American landscape is dotted with monuments to the sacrifices of the Civil War. In our churches, when a building project is completed, a cornerstone and sometimes a time capsule are put in place as a way of telling the story to those who may someday take the building for granted. When a family member has made the transition into glory, a stone monument is placed upon his or her grave, sometimes with an epitaph sharing a bit of that person's wisdom with those who visit the spot.

The next step in your church's transition will be to take stock of these messages from the past. Going into the Reverse step means involving the congregation in a fresh exploration of its history as well as its denominational heritage. This step may seem counterintuitive; but until we look in the mirror and back up, our history haunts us. When a church is stuck, there is always something blocking forward progress. Trying to rev up the engine and plow through will only dig you in deeper because momentum is not working with you. In taking a brief trip into the past, we can come to terms with our history. This task needs to be done on three levels: Celebration, Study, and Intervention.

Celebration

The first level of the Reverse step involves the entire congregation in some type of history celebration. The celebration may be a fun event, such as an anniversary celebration or "old home day." It may also be a series of vignettes during the worship service, or newsletter articles that bring to light the personalities and events of both the congregation's own history and the history of their faith tradition. These activities support the congregation's work in discovering a positive self-identity that will remain with them after the transition. If there has been a change in pastors, that event is a vehicle for the congregation to share its story with the incoming pastor.

Most congregations find reconnecting with their past to be an energizing experience. Every congregation has a multitude of inspirational tidbits in its archives. Unfortunately many of these stories are unrecorded and in danger of being lost as aged members pass away. Done well, programs focused on history send the congregation on a scavenger hunt through the memories of their often silent elderly. The laughter ensues as events are relived and portrayed in worship or other fellowship gatherings. Remembering the local church's story also provides opportunity for reconnecting with the deeper traditions of the larger church and your denominational history. These comforting and inspirational stories provide a welcome respite in the otherwise arduous journey of transition.

Study

The second, deeper level of the Reverse step is serious study within the Pilot Group and other leadership teams to discover linkages between the church's past, present, and potential future. This study begins with the group creating a timeline of the church's life. This timeline can be publicly displayed, perhaps on a strip of butcher paper running along a wall in a fellowship hall or meeting space. The Pilot Group, however, needs to feel free to annotate and stick notes on the timeline. The timeline is not a work of art, but rather it is a working drawing for reconstructing the congregation's sense of self-identity. As the transition progresses, this timeline will be returned to again and again as new insights accumulate. The timeline provides a perspective for understanding the changes that are occurring within the congregation.

Those viewing the timeline should feel free to draw connections between the cultural context of the church and how successful various choices made by the church in the past have been. The study groups engaged in this task should be mindful of Santayana's warning that "those who cannot remember the past are condemned to repeat it."[1] The truth is, in fact, a bit worse. We not only will repeat the mistakes of previous generations when we lose touch with our history, but will also fail to receive encouragement and guidance from their successes.

Intervention

The third level of the Reverse step involves the honest appraisal and acceptance of recent events. Here we seek to intervene and break the cycles and conflicts that have kept the church from her work. Interim ministers are trained to spend time hearing and affirming the recent history of a congregation. In Chapter 14 we will look at the dysfunctional communication patterns that may have developed within the congregation. At this level the Pilot Group needs to demonstrate how clear communication enabled the church to do great things in the past. Where and how has the leadership of the church strayed from integrity and "speaking the truth in love" (Ephesians 4:15)?

It is important to see history as something that cannot be changed, but history can be healed. Treated responsibly, even the most devastating events of the past become valuable life lessons. If there has been trauma in the life of the parish, it is irresponsible to simply sweep the matter under the rug. During the transition period the church leadership pledges to ask the question, What do we need to do so that all parties involved find closure? Just as individuals can repress psychological pain, hurting congregations can bury unpleasant events under "no-talk" rules. Unresolved issues tap the congregation's energy and foster hidden agendas among church leaders. Until we exhume such skeletons, every effort to move forward is thwarted.

In seeking to display our history and speak about it, we bring about healing when we

- provide recognition to those who may have made unnoticed contributions in the past;
- become aware of and accepting of our diversity and ethnic and theological differences viewed against the backdrop of a greater history;
- note how our predecessors overcame challenges, thus giving our problems a sense of perspective;
- speak about our hurts and enable ourselves to progress toward forgiveness;
- become more able to center on the present moment.

The important thing about spending time discussing and displaying congregational history is that it enables the past to be left in the past. We accept that various people may have different feelings about what happened in the past, but together we recognize that the past is the past. In affirming that prior pastors were unique individuals, we free ourselves from the tendency to expect current clergy to be their clones. Giving sufficient credit to past accomplishments allows people to accept change as a part of life.

When congregational history is done properly, the church's sense of identity is strengthened. People learn to value the church for what it is in itself rather than because it has a certain program or building or cherished pastor. This reaffirmation of the church's true identity is important, especially since the transition process may lead toward changes in pastoral leadership, church property, or the abandonment of programs that are no longer needed.

Congregational Secrets

When Reverend Wiseman began serving old first church, he noticed that his congregation was rather formal during the "passing of the peace" time of the worship service. They rarely went in for more than a quick handshake with immediate neighbors. His previous congregation had to be called back to worship after a raucous seven minutes of hugging and greeting in the main aisle.

It was a year and a half later before a chance remark revealed a deep congregational secret. A letter of transfer arrived for a member wishing to join a nearby church. When Reverend Wiseman asked his membership secretary if she knew why this family had left the church, she responded that the father of the family had been asked to leave. Finally the story came out about an usher who had groped a number of the women of the congregation. He had a habit of giving a hug when he handed out a bulletin, but sometimes his hug went further than the congregation felt comfortable with. "I told him to keep his hands to himself and he left me alone," the membership secretary offered.

Reverend Wiseman knew that he had just been told something that would explain much of the resistance he had experienced toward making the worship experience more casual. Typical of most congregational secrets, this one was common knowledge among everybody except those who needed to know.

Churches, like most families, tend to deal with the misbehavior of individuals through private channels. As in the case of the usher above, the former pastor handled the matter by calling the man into his office and requesting him to step down from his role as usher. This pastor was relieved to see the man discretely choose to relocate his family into another church rather than face public embarrassment. The incident became a secret, subtly influencing the behavior of many within the congregation. Since it was resolved without conflict, no one thought it necessary to discuss it with the new pastor.

Reverend Wiseman, however, found himself wrestling with how he, as a pastor and worship leader, could gradually move the congregation toward feeling less vulnerable when they expressed signs of Christian love and fellowship with one another.

Remembering history, especially while in a period of transition, often uncovers congregational secrets. The point is not to air every piece of dirty laundry in public. Some incidents need to be discussed discretely among those who have a legitimate need to know. Other events need to be aired where prayer and theological reflection can be called upon to bring about healing. Still other incidents clearly call for the church council to take action and establish procedures that will safeguard the church from future misconduct.

Just as there are times when old skeletons need to be brought out of the closet, so also there are times when church leaders need to adopt an attitude that is more respectful of the rights of individuals to privacy. Many congregations fail to grant sufficient personal

Giving sufficient credit to past accomplishments allows people to accept change as a part of life.

space and privacy to the pastor and the pastor's family. Churches are legally and morally responsible for maintaining confidentiality related to employee records as well as certain items on job application files. One of the duties of the Pilot Group during transition is to investigate whether a failure in respecting personal boundaries has contributed to the church's current level of conflict. What new policies need to be developed to insure that the church leadership works within the boundaries of confidentiality? that individuals and groups strengthen their respect for personal privacy?

Often members of prayer chains and fellowship groups will engage in destructive sharing of private information. Sometimes clergy and church secretaries can be too glib in sharing items that they learned in confidence. Every person has a right to expect that information about health conditions or family conflicts will not be revealed without their expressed permission. Restoring public confidence in the church's ability to be a therapeutic organization requires careful planning about how and when secrets will be shared.

For Discussion

1. Recall incidents that have been defining moments for you. Talk to the group about how these events shaped your personality, your occupational choice, or your attitude toward life's goals.

2. What have you done to recover your own roots? Have you participated in a family genealogy project? Have reunions, weddings, and funerals been for your family an occasion for reminiscing and sharing family lore? Are there traditions or family stories that you have been careful to share with the next generation?

3. On a scale of one to ten, how familiar are you with the history of your local church?

   1   2   3   4   5   6   7   8   9   10
   (hardly aware)   (very informed)

4. On a scale of one to ten, how familiar are you with the history of your denomination?

   1   2   3   4   5   6   7   8   9   10
   (hardly aware)   (very informed)

5. In reflecting upon the story of Reverend Wiseman and the usher accused of sexual misconduct, how do you think your own church would handle a similar incident?

6. Do you feel that handling congregational secrets will be an important issue for the transition process?

7. Have the church council and the committee on pastor/staff-parish relations received sufficient training and resources to assess and reduce the church's vulnerability to cases of sexual harassment and leadership misconduct? errors in counseling provided by the pastor and others? financial misconduct? endangerment of children and youth? cases involving the wrongful termination of employees?

8. Should the church council work to develop new policies that will strengthen confidentiality and respect for personal privacy in the church?

9. In general, on which side of the secrecy/confidentiality balance is your congregation likely to err?
   • Too much secrecy. Things are swept under the rug.
   • Too little respect for individual privacy. Gossip runs rampant.

Endnote

1 *The Life of Reason*, by George Santayana, 1905–1906.

Chapter 14
Dysfunctional Communication

In the "Mapping Linkages" exercise in Chapter 9, we looked at how the whole church is linked together by lines of communication and influence. Being able to see the church as a dynamic system of relationships is an important step in the transition process. While in Park, we tried to get a general overview of the church as a system, noting the places where conflict currently exists. Now review your map and count the number of links that are healthy (marked by normal lines ——) and the number that are broken or improperly related (dashed - - - -; broken —/ /—; double ═══; or jagged /\/\/\).

Even if the ratio of healthy to unhealthy is rather high, such as nine good relationships for every problematic one, there is still reason for concern. Since the church is a system, broken and dysfunctional links between people and committees not only disrupt the tasks they share but also foster an imbalance that is felt throughout the whole system. The more conflicted individual relationships become, the more people throughout the organization will respond defensively by reducing and dropping their current relationships. People will act more and more in isolation. Committees will not pause to consider how their actions affect the work of others in the church. Often there will be a drop in attendance or enthusiasm at the church council level because the committee chairs resent having to present their ideas for approval by the whole body. No one trusts the system.

The balance and harmony we long for in our church is dependent upon clear communication between groups and leaders. But communication in an organization cannot happen unless there is a spirit of fair play and trust. Can we present our own ideas and values to the group, trusting that they will be judged purely upon their own merit? Can we listen when someone expresses a different point of view? Will politics or an ongoing conflict color each interaction or inhibit the needed exchange of information between committees?

Whenever individuals distrust an organization's ability to respond to their feelings and ideas fairly, they shut down and engage in defensive styles of communication. Instead of openly expressing themselves to the person who needs their input, they ricochet their comments off a third party (called *triangulation*) or falsely express their opinions and make concessions, only to lash out when they can embarrass the other party (*passive-aggressive behavior*). These defensive mechanisms entangle communication while building a protective wall around the individual or committees. An honest map of the organization's leadership structure would look like a medieval landscape, dotted with fortresses protecting individual fiefdoms. Nothing productive or wholesome happens in a church that is stuck in the Dark Ages in terms of their interpersonal relationships.

While triangulation and passive-aggressive behavior are but two of many defenses that disrupt communication, their frequency in the church merits closer attention. If the Pilot Group and church council can discuss and agree to root out these barriers to the flow of ideas, the change initiatives developed in the Drive step will have a greater chance of taking root.

Triangulation in Communication

Triangulation occurs when one person uses another person to convey a message to or exercise some type of control over a third person. Many of us have experienced or participated in triangulation in our families. A father may disapprove of his teenage daughter's latest boyfriend. Instead of speaking directly to her about his concerns, he manipulates his wife into intervening with her. Although the mother may have no negative feelings about the boyfriend, taking on this peacemaker role may become habitual for her. She may think she knows why the father is upset, but what if she cannot precisely convey this to her daughter? However skillfully she states the issue, the mother's own feelings are lost in the process. The daughter is unlikely to know what parts of the message are coming from Mom and what parts involve the relationship she has with her father. Further, the daughter is unlikely to respond to the message or seek clarification about its content from her father. Venting to her mother, or another third party, seems normal. Since the message came to her indirectly, why shouldn't she respond by involving more people in the conflict on her side. The anxiety level in the family is raised as messages bounce off of more and more auxiliary individuals before they reach their targets.

The more triangulation is employed in a family, the more confused each member becomes about his or her own role and relationships. Even simple messages become jumbled when they are passed through a third party. The father may think he is defusing the possibility of the daughter blowing up by using the mother as a mediator. If, however, he cannot build integrity into the negative encounters he has with his daughter, the whole opportunity for a meaningful relationship is compromised. The mother may not be aware of how disruptive triangulation is for her own relationship with her daughter. If she is constantly mediating the feelings of others, how will people know when she is speaking for herself?

Jesus shows his concern about the effects of triangulation on the church when he lays down rules for settling disputes. He says,

> If another member of the church sins against you, go and point out the fault when the two of you are alone. If the member listens to you, you have regained that one.
>
> (Matthew 18:15)

In every church there are laypeople who use triangulation through the pastor as a way to express their opinion. Instead of interacting with those people who are responsible for choices, such as the color of carpet in the narthex or the location of a meeting, they pull the reverend over to their corner and complain in his or her ear. The expectation, whether it is openly expressed or not, is that it is the pastor's job to carry these reports to the appropriate party. When pastors fall into this trap, they shift the communication pattern of the congregation. Soon anything that needs to be said from one committee to another will be routed through the pastor. Unfortunately, many pastors see themselves as mediators and are sympathetic when someone asks them to speak on their behalf to another party. They become willing parties in triangulation, hoping to smooth over and prevent conflict between opposing parties. The truth is, all triangulation breaks communication, denigrates the messenger (in this case the pastor), and raises the level of anxiety surrounding the situation.

There is another form of triangulation that occurs when people complain among themselves rather than approaching the pastor or other leader who is directly responsible for some incident. Pastors are often aware of the murmurings of discontent in their congregation, but they are unable to sufficiently identify the core issues. They may respond by working harder, but in the wrong area. An active clique of complainers may be sharing their concerns about the pastor's failure to visit key shut-ins. Missing this message but fearing that his ministry is slipping, the pastor responds by devoting more of his time to

Triangulation occurs when one person uses another person to convey a message to or exercise some type of control over a third person.

sermon preparation or youth work. Without direct communication it is hard for anyone in church leadership to respond to problems.

Finally, pastors and other church leaders may themselves be guilty of traveling the low road of triangulation rather than directly communicating with their flock. When you are unsure how someone will react, or when you doubt your own capacity to state your case, it is tempting to recruit a go-between to act for you. Some pastors use their sermons as an instrument for indirectly expressing their disapproval of an individual's or group's actions. This form of triangulation demeans the worship service, making the sermon a mediator for thoughts and feelings the pastor is unwilling to express directly to those involved. For all church leaders, failure to communicate directly invites confusion and may be an inappropriate use of authority.

Passive-Aggressive Behavior

Like triangulation, we may experience passive-aggressive behavior frequently in our own families. This behavior occurs when a person who has resources or authority in a situation does not clearly express his or her unwillingness to support or grant permission for another person's idea or action. The person may withhold funding or information needed by the other person. The passive-aggressive person seems to say yes but then finds subtle ways to sabotage the event. For example, a parent may concede to a teenager's request to get a driver's permit but then fail to provide opportunities for the teenager to practice driving. If after many delays they go out on the road, the parent berates the kid's ability to handle the car. The passive-aggressive person may appear to be supportive. In the end, though, that person rigs the situation with so much negative energy that the other person fails to get what was understood to be possible. The teenager, in this example, fails to learn to drive. The parent tells others, "I tried to teach him, but he wasn't ready."

Committees and church leaders who practice passive-aggressive behavior are often accused of playing games, forcing others to jump through hoops, or using indifference to intimidate and control. They may even obstruct events and programs that lie outside of their direct control. For example, a church member who disapproves of a scout group using the facility may "accidentally" cause the group to be locked out or left without heat on the night of their meetings. Pastors have a great deal of opportunity to starve the programs that they dislike by simply failing to provide needed information and connection to the church's resources. Most pastors, on the other hand, have experienced a time when a church board gave tacit approval to a pet project only to undermine the process in a passive-aggressive manner.

Passive-aggressive behavior is a false communication pattern that leads to frustration, confusion, and failure to meet the agreed-upon objectives and goals of an organization. Like other systemic problems, it has a tendency to spread until people habitually choose to express their disapproval with passive resistance instead of honest dialogue. It may be necessary to confront this tendency whenever we observe

- unexpected procrastination
- the withholding of needed information
- mixed messages or vague expectations
- leaders sitting on the fence about issues
- people being deceptive about their own needs and wishes
- unexpected displays of anger when things succeed
- defensive separation or rejoicing when things fail

Passive-aggressive behavior occurs when a person who has resources or authority in a situation does not clearly express his or her unwillingness to support another person's idea or action.

Besides calling such behavior into question, the church leadership who is striving for honest communication must

- be clear about what will occur if a program is given approval to proceed
- set boundaries to prevent obstruction by other parties
- confront ambiguous information or comments
- agree to reasonable timelines for actions and question procrastination
- get parties to covenant support for whatever actions are approved at church meetings

For Discussion

1. Does the number or quality of relationships between committees and key church leaders in your church cause you concern? Which particular relationships would you like to see improved?

2. If each broken or damaged link in a system causes an imbalance in the whole, then each repaired relationship has great potential in terms of bringing healing to the whole. What tools is the transition process giving you to bring about healing in your church?

3. Talk about or note an example of triangulation from your everyday life.

4. Small groups with five to fifteen members may experiment with the "passing secrets" game. A simple message, such as, "Harry was sent to the store for canned beans, ice cream, and a newspaper," is whispered into one group member's ear. That person passes the message to the person on his or her right. The message continues to be passed from person to person around the group. The final message is compared with the original. Most groups find that the final message bears no comparison to the first. Using the engineering concept of signal to noise, each new person added to a stream of communication doubles the noise (the amount of untrue information) and halves the signal (the content of the original message). How does this affect the clarity of communication when triangulation is involved?

5. Why do people who are asked to carry messages from one person to another often feel denigrated and de-energized by the process?

6. Talk about or note an example of passive-aggressive behavior from your everyday life.

7. Where are you concerned about the effect of passive-aggressive behavior on the relational linkages of your church? Has the church council or another significant body in the church ever begun a new program, activity, or procedure only to have it blocked by one or two individuals or a powerful group in the church?

8. Has a pastor ever starved a church program or process by benign neglect?

9. How might the passive-aggressive behavior of church members be a significant factor in causing clergy burnout?

Chapter 15

Programs for Doing History

Most churches "do history" in an irreverent manner. They nonchalantly stash excess church records on the third floor, where they form a barrier to the more interesting vintage photographs and memorabilia. They ask the oldest member to be the church historian but provide no mechanism for that person to pass information on to the next generation. This benign neglect fosters the mistaken notion that a church's past is an obstacle rather than an inspiration for the challenges and changes she will encounter in the future.

When a congregation feels lost in the midst of the terrain of conflict and transition, looking at history is like referring to a map. We begin by finding where we are in the landscape of change. Looking back into our recent past we see the turns and traumatic events that brought us to this place. Looking further back we see that we are but a small part of a larger story. Regaining this sense of perspective renews our hope in the God who acts in history.

The "Church Timeline" is a physical map that is drawn to reveal and put on the table the intangible aspects of the congregation's history. The Pilot Group will be modifying and referring to the timeline in several of the following chapters, but the actual timeline can be created and appreciated by the whole congregation. Some churches assign the timeline task to the people or committee in the church most interested in history. The project can be unveiled and interpreted at a fellowship dinner or other event during the Reverse step of the transition. The Pilot Group, however, will need to find a way to attach its own information to the timeline. These attachments might involve additional strips of paper or adhesive notes.

> When a congregation feels lost in the midst of the terrain of conflict and transition, looking at history is like referring to a map.

Exercise: The Church Timeline

1. Choose an accessible location in the church with at least ten feet of clear wall space, such as the fellowship hall or narthex. The completed timeline will hang for several months throughout the Reverse step of the transition period. The more visible the timeline is to the whole congregation the better.

2. Hang a long strip of butcher paper the full length of the space. (Alternatively, a series of cork boards or fabric could be stretched to form the backdrop for the timeline.)

3. Mark at the far left end of the strip the founding date of the congregation. Draw a horizontal line across the middle of the strip and distribute vertical time tics on a regular basis along it. Leave about two feet of blank space past the present mark of the timeline. If the church has a history of over seventy-five years, you may wish to label larger quarter-century time tics as well as marking each decade. If the church has not been around that long, then you are free to make the decades the major tics

and label the individual years. Some accommodation may be made for the fact that more details will be noted in the last ten years. In fact, this section may be expanded in a separate section.

4. Mark above the timeline the significant events of world and local history. These should include the wars that involved our nation, technological events such as the Wright Brothers' flight in 1903 and the moon landing in 1969, and denominational mergers and events in the larger church's history. Was there a major new highway constructed near the church that affected the neighborhood? Was the church involved in the civil rights movement or affected by a labor dispute? What about natural disasters? What have been the most significant changes in your town or region?

5. Attach photos, newspaper clippings, and graphics to illuminate the social setting of the church in the midst of history.

6. Mark below the timeline the significant events of the congregation's life. When have various building projects been completed? Attach before and after photographs where possible. What have been the proudest moments and the darkest ones for the church. Are there photos available for missionaries or special projects that the church supported? Who has gone into the ministry from this congregation?

7. Across the bottom of the strip, note the ministries of the church's pastors. Have any of these people gone on to serve higher offices in the church? Are there things about their style of ministry that can be remembered and placed like graffiti above their name?

8. Go back and attempt to fill in the blank spots of the chart. Humorous and poignant remembrances should be scattered throughout the timeline. Use group photos and memorabilia from church activities. The idea is to make the timeline an extended scrapbook of the life of the congregation.

9. Hang near the beginning of the timeline a poster displaying the history of the larger church going back to Christ and showing the history of your denomination. This poster can often be assembled from material found in confirmation class curriculum.

Options for Using the Timeline

• Use the timeline as a fellowship activity following worship or a pot-luck supper. Hang the timeline and have the time periods marked before people arrive. Gather the church history materials and markers, but let the congregation do the actual research and placement.

• Place the timeline on the church's Internet web page and invite participation via e-mail. Each week, post the additional dates and remembrances contributed.

• Post the timeline in or near the worship space and add material each week. Be sure to do numbers 1 through 3 early in the Reverse step or even before it begins. The next five items can then be done one each week, building interest in the project.

• Reproduce the results of numbers 1, 2, 3, and 7 on several sheets of paper for the Pilot Team to use separately.

Other Reverse Programs

In conjunction with the congregational timeline, here are some other ways to engage the congregation in a rediscovery of their history.

Old Home Week

Old Home Week is a weeklong or weekend-long celebration of the church's heritage. Denominational officials and former pastors are invited to speak. Members who have moved away are given a special invitation to return and be recognized. The worship service focuses on the glories of the church both past and present.

A special fellowship meal is planned. Afterward someone can present a lighthearted look at the church's past. Come up with a "top ten" list of the funniest things that have happened in the church or at church functions. Do not include anything that would embarrass anyone; when in doubt ask permission. You may also want to have an actor portray a key figure in the church's history as part of the evening's entertainment.

Weekly History Moments

Present each of the four previous eras of your church during five to ten minutes in worship on four Sundays. This "Historical Moment" can be presented as a skit or as a short informative talk. If the church has access to PowerPoint, this is an excellent time to use modern technology to teach about the church's past.

As with the other church history programs, give some attention to the history of the larger church and your denomination. Be sure to investigate how your faith tradition was introduced to your region. Did your local church play a significant role in the spread of faith into your vicinity?

Talent Show

Invite the members of the congregation to prepare to present a talent or fun skit at a talent show. Encourage people to show unusual or gag talents. Part of the purpose of the event is to be fun, generating energy needed for the first half of transition. Include in this show reflections of the congregation's history by

- creating vignettes to put talents of the church's membership—past and present—on display. Who has given a particular talent to the church over many faithful years of service? This may be the opportunity to recognize the organist, the fix-it man, or the church cook for special contributions.

- writing skits portraying characters out of the church's history;

- preparing a slide show of photos taken at recent church activities.

The message is that everyone in the church is talented and the church is a great place to use our talents together.

Church Tour

Organize a stained-glass window and memorial tour of your church. Be sure to print a brochure that will enable those who miss the event to do the walk at their own leisure. There is often a great deal of history in the objects and furnishings of the church. Many members may be unaware of when additions were made to the church facilities and why.

Investigative History

Just as small groups may set aside their usual curriculum to take time to consider the church's purpose, the transition process is supported when classes take an interest in the historical background of the congregation. Some classes may enjoy working through the primary source material of church records and memorabilia in an attempt to write their own church history or to organize a display in the church narthex. Other classes may choose to study a unit on denominational or early church history. Sunday school classes can use this topic for one quarter by studying the Book of Acts in the first half of the quarter and then doing four or five lessons on the history of the post-New Testament church.

For children's and youth classes, the teachers should be aware that church history is rarely sufficiently covered during the preparation of young people for church membership.

Round out their education by using some of the Sunday school class time to introduce them to key figures such as St. Augustine, Martin Luther, John Wesley, Dietrich Bonhoeffer, and Martin Luther King, Jr. If in the same process the teachers devote some attention to the founders of their own local congregation, children and youth will come to see themselves as connected to the ongoing work of God's Holy Spirit.

Chapter 16
Denominational Heritage

When traumatic events rock a local church, the relationship between the congregation and its denomination often becomes frayed. If the conflict is related to perceived pastoral misconduct or incompetence, there will be those who blame the denomination or regional association for sending the pastor. This hostility is present even in churches that have a congregational polity that allows the local church to select its own candidate for pastor. The fact that the church members at one time enthusiastically received this person does not negate the impulse to seek a scapegoat for the mistake in the denominational home office. "Someone higher up should have known this would happen" is a common lament among those in churches experiencing leadership trauma. Since financial difficulties often accompany transition, members tend to resent their mission assessments and denominational obligations. There may be an impatient cry from the church officers, "Why can't they (the conference or judicatory) help us out now, after all the money we have sent them over the years?"

Whether the fault lies with the denominational office or not, any hostility toward the larger church is counterproductive to the transition process. As long as a congregation simmers in the blame game, they will continue to respond reactively to their problems rather than intentionally seeking proactive ways to live with change. When we assume that our problems come down to us from above, we also assume that all the answers and the power belong with the hierarchy. Making constructive progress through transition is dependent upon getting the church leaders to search for the answers to the church's problems within the congregation and its own sense of mission.

The church needs to get out of the mode of holding its breath while waiting for the denomination to send the perfect pastor. Those who make financial decisions or who are responsible for the church's stewardship drive need to act rather than sit and complain that the regional office is not bailing them out. Rather than moving in the direction of becoming more co-dependent upon denominational officials, the church needs to reconnect with its roots and form an interdependent relationship with other churches of its religious tradition. When the church emerges at the other end of the transition process, it will find itself with a new healthy sense of self-respect and identity within its own religious heritage.

While the answers to all the church's problems will not come in the form of a gift from the denominational hierarchy, the transition period is an important time to rediscover the resources that your denomination may provide to help your church toward greater health. As in the old saying, the purpose of the denominational office is not to provide you with a fish every day but rather to teach you how to fish.

Some ways the denominational office may provide support for the transition period are by

- providing consultants and interim clergy for the transition process;
- being a source for materials on recovering from various forms of church leadership trauma;

> Any hostility toward the larger church is counter-productive to the transition process.

- providing risk assessment tools and samples of policies that may protect the local church from future trauma;

- providing loans and grants for startup of new programs and building projects;

- providing training for the church members on how to write grants and seek community improvement funding;

- connecting the church leaders with local demographic data and other resources that will help them make proactive choices about future ministries;

- connecting congregations with other congregations for mutually beneficial projects.

For Discussion

1. Talk about or note your own concerns about your denomination's involvement in each of these areas:

   - Theological issues: Where is the denomination leading the local churches in terms of understanding God and God's will for people?

   - Clergy training: What is the denomination doing to recruit and equip people who are called to the professional ministry?

   - Support of local and global missions: How does the denomination organize mission work and distribute the funds raised by the church for the needs of others?

   - Clergy oversight and placement: How does the denomination supervise its clergy? What concerns do you have about the way clergy are placed in the local church?

2. How would you rate your local church's relationship with the denominational office and the officials most immediately concerned with her welfare? (Circle the most appropriate answer.)

   Distant   Poor   Average   Fair   Good   Excellent

3. What can be done to improve your congregation's perception of the denomination?

Chapter 17
Evaluating Your History

The purpose of the timeline is not simply to invoke nostalgia but to provide a record of how change has affected the life of the congregation. When a person is recovering from a heart attack, part of rehabilitation involves reviewing the lifestyle of the past. Stress, diet, exercise, blood pressure, weight, and the intake of calories and fats are evaluated. Changes are prescribed to move in the right direction in the future. The Pilot Group and others must evaluate and learn from the church's timeline. During transition a church not only recognizes and recovers from the effects of a traumatic change but also makes plans and institutes intentional changes so that she can be a vibrant fellowship in the future.

Doing the Numbers

Go back to the church timeline and place below each time tic the average number of attendees at all worship services. For the most recent period, chart this number for each year. Then go to every five years for the next twenty-five years back, and to every ten years for the decades from there back to the church's beginning. This information is normally available from the statistical reports that clergy are required to file each year. If local church records are not available, your denominational office may have statistical journals. As you reach further back into history, you may need to do rough approximations based on the remembrances of the elderly on how full the church was. The idea is to gather enough data to be able to note those periods where there have been significant changes. Since the congregation was formed, what is the overall trend in terms of attendance?

A graph of the statistics of average worship attendance over the decades may be worth a thousand words. The Pilot Group should return to the church timeline and place self-adhesive notes at every location where the attendance figure changed by more than twenty percent. Then look both above and below the central timeline and discuss what was happening outside and inside the church during that time to cause the change in worship attendance. Was there any period in the church's life that could be called "a golden era"?

Many church growth experts recommend charting worship attendance, church school attendance, and membership. These numbers will provide an even more accurate picture. With an average of these three numbers, membership reflects the congregation's past, and church school attendance indicates something of future strength. Worship attendance is a more volatile reflection of the present, being altered by factors such as the congregation's first impressions of a new pastor or the way the current usher counts heads.

Some will ask why numbers are important at all. While statistics do not show a church's spiritual fervor, resilience, or potential for future growth, they do indicate current health. Each digit represents a person who has turned to this church for spiritual support and training in his or her task of being a Christian disciple. When the numbers fall, fewer people are finding what they need at this location. When Jesus called the church to make disciples, he was giving her a purpose that was numerically quantifiable. He could have said, "Go make people feel better about God." Such a task would be vague enough for us to forget all about numbers. As it is, though, Jesus gave us a purpose that is directly related to numbers, such as church attendance.

Size Boundaries

Saw shape

Undulating hills

Stair step

Steps up and down

Looking at your graph of church attendance over the years, what shape do the numbers form? Is there a steady rise in attendance or a decline? Few churches have a simple up or down graph. Some have a saw shape chart or a set of undulating hills. Many churches have a staircase, where there has been growth up to a plateau and then a long stretch of no growth or slight decline. Then something happens and they grow again. In each case of staircase growth for your church, what was the thing that happened to precipitate growth?

Some churches have steps up and down. The important thing to note is that every change in direction is a transitional moment. Churches may experience growth without thinking about transition or the issues that this change thrusts upon them. Sooner or later the new reality of what it means to fulfill our purpose as a larger church needs to be addressed. If transitional issues are not resolved, a church will reach a plateau and stop growing.

If the church has declined in the recent past and then leveled off, there will often be church traditions, attitudes, and policies that were more appropriate for the former size of the church. Such reminders of past times are like the ghost sensations that a recent amputee experiences in that they imagine themselves feeling the fingers or toes of the departed limb. When the church transitions down to a smaller size, it is important that they go through a process of rediscovering their purpose and evaluating programs and ministries to ensure that they align with their new sense of identity.

Theories of Church Growth and Decline

Why is it that churches grow up to a certain point then plateau or decline? There are three general theories that explain this universal phenomenon. Let's look at three: systems theory, facility limitations, and size-identity barriers.

Systems Theory

Systems theory was alluded to in Chapter 9, "Leadership Interdependence," and in Chapter 14, "Dysfunctional Communication." If we assume that the church is an interdependent system of communication links and relationships, then a growing church needs to constantly add new links and improve the relationships between church leaders. New people with talents and time to give to church work need to be incorporated into the system. At some point, though, the system collapses or fails to ensure good linkages between people. Triangulation or passive-aggressive behavior becomes more frequent. The church leaders stop sharing their ideas freely with one another, and newcomers to the congregation cease feeling invited into the decision-making process. Soon nobody trusts the system.

A church that wants to keep growing must keep evaluating its leadership connections. What can be done to maximize the healthy interaction between committees? When recent attendees become a part of the congregation, how long is it before they are assimilated into church leadership? The tendency in most growing organisms is to develop layers of hierarchy. This means that people who are new to the church have fewer meaningful connections and may have less contact with the pastor and other significant leaders.

To keep growing, churches must keep reinventing their organization to eliminate hierarchy. They must intentionally value the contributions of newcomers. As we saw back in Chapter 8, valuing innovation and improving listening skills are key tasks for church leaders when the church is in transition. The problems that the church faces as it adapts to a new size are usually solved by those who have recently joined the church and are free from the constraints of the old way of seeing things. If church committee structure and decision-making process can remain boundary-less (see pages 40–41), then the number of those participating in the church will continue to grow as the church grows. This flexibility, however, depends on the pastor and other key leaders teaching that the process of making decisions and involving fresh insights from newcomers is more important than having any particular decision made the way we want it.

Another term for this process of being ready to reinvent the organization is to call it new learning. When a child comes home from school, parents may ask, "What did you learn new today?" The emphasis is not on accumulated facts, but upon new learning. Somewhere in early adulthood we make a shift; we start resting on what we already know. Having and acting upon existing information becomes more important than keeping curious and open to new ways of learning. But what happens if we suddenly get laid off? In today's world many are finding that their job skills are no longer marketable. The only way to survive is to retrain and to develop an attitude that says, "You're never too old to learn." For the church, transition is always a process of new learning.

Whether a church is making an upward transition or becoming smaller, being flexible is critical. Church leaders need to be willing to adapt the ways things are organized and done in the church to match new realities. A church of a certain size may get away with having a relatively formal and hierarchal structure; but if during transition it becomes a smaller church, that way of doing things will become totally inappropriate. Stuck on the old way of doing things, the leaders may continue to fund ministries and schedule programs that are poorly attended. Without an emphasis on new learning, an organization lacks the courage to cut its losses and strike out in new directions.

Facility Limitations

Many churches grow only as far as they were designed to grow. They are like a houseplant that is able to reach only a certain size because it reaches the limit of its pot. To grow any further, the plant needs a bigger space for its roots. For the church, space limitations can involve one or more of the following issues:

• not enough parking space

• limited worship seating and comfort

• increased need for ministry or program space

• accessibility issues

Sometimes these issues become intertwined and expensive to address. Building committees, church planting organizations, and the architects of the past century had no way of envisioning how their design and location choices would place numerical limitations upon the church's final size.

One urban church entered a major building campaign to provide a gym (program space for children and youth ministries) as well as an elevator and a new lobby area (accessibility issues). During the construction phase for the new building they also purchased housing and provided some new parking space. The church that had been averaging 150 in worship attendance soon found itself approaching 200 but never quite able to surpass this number.

Church leaders were also aware that worship comfort might be a factor limiting their growth. The local fire marshal had closed the balcony that no longer met code, and a recent sanctuary renovation project further reduced the sanctuary seating from a maximum of 250 to just under 200. Some church growth research seems to indicate that a church pew feels uncomfortable to a newcomer when it is about 80 percent full. People first entering a sanctuary where fewer than 20 percent of the seats are available to them may wonder if the

Church leaders need to be willing to adapt the ways things are organized and done in the church to match new realities.

church has room for them. For this church, the limit of comfortable seating was about 160. This problem was further complicated by the fact that the overflow seating space (folding chairs) was usually taken over by the music and drama department on holidays.

In order to address this need, an earlier worship service was added. The earliness of the hour as well as the church's traditional emphasis on high quality music at the later service kept this service's popularity down to less than a quarter of the later service. Because the majority of people also attended Sunday school, which met between the two services, the new service did not significantly help the parking problem. On holidays, when most new attendees do their church shopping, attendance at the later service was still over 200, with latecomers being accommodated on folding chairs in the aisle. Comfort may well have been placing a ceiling on this church's growth.

Another comfort issue the church needed to address was the lack of air conditioning. The church was located in a region that only exceeded eighty degrees a dozen Sundays a year; cooling had never been a high priority. However, even though the impact of air conditioning is hard to measure, people seem less willing to sacrifice comfort today. Maybe the fact that every other place people gather is air-conditioned has changed what people consider to be normal.

The parking issue returned with a vengeance when Main Street was widened and the church's access to on-street parking was eliminated. Longtime churchgoers quickly found alternate parking on side streets. The church's long-term planning team, however, could see the trends that would make purchasing land for additional parking a major concern for the future. As one team member said, "Twenty-five years ago, half our members walked to church. Today, not more than three families walk on any given Sunday. To make matters worse, many of our families drive two or more cars to church because of their involvement in different classes, worship services, and after-church activities."

Looking at how the demands the congregation places on the church's facilities have changed over the years can be an eye-opening experience. As you look back over your timeline, consider the items on the "Checklist for the Church Facility," page 81.

Size-Identity Barriers

At the same time the church described above was hitting physical facilities barriers, the church was also undergoing a transition in terms of the quality and types of programs the congregation expected to be offered by the church. When a church nears 200 in average worship attendance, a subtle shift occurs in its self-identity. When they are a smaller church, having everyone march to the beat of the same drum is acceptable. When they grow larger, different strokes for different folks becomes the watchword.

The following shifts were in motion long before this church reached 200:

- The church offered additional worship services so that those with different tastes and time schedules could be accommodated. The church eventually developed a third worship service with a contemporary flavor on Saturdays.

- The pastor was no longer able or expected to attend every church event. Much of what happened in the church began happening without the pastor's input.

- A full-time staff person was hired to operate the new ministries in the gym. For a time, an associate pastor with a different theological bent from the senior pastor was given the freedom to develop new programs for the church.

- The leadership structure of the church was altered so that many volunteers were connected to the structure and supervised by the program staff rather than by the senior pastor.

The size transition of moving from 175 to 225 in average attendance is far more challenging to a congregation's self-identity than the transition from 125 to 175. Growing past

Checklist for the Church Facility

What pressures, like the preference for air conditioning, are you experiencing because society has changed the expectations people have for public buildings?

Monitor the parking for several Sundays. Are easily found spaces available for late-comers to each of the scheduled events? What do you think happens on holidays?

What number was your sanctuary originally designed to seat? At what points on the timeline were changes made to your church's seating capacity?

How many people are in each car? Family size has shrunk, and the number of cars per giving unit has increased. Each parking space may represent two thousand dollars lost to the church's yearly budget if that family chooses to go elsewhere.

Is your current attendance more than eighty percent of your total seating capacity? What happens during the peak holiday Sundays?

Has your congregation seen a rise in the attendance and involvement of people with disabilities over the last two decades? If so, this is due to both the rising average age of churchgoers and a shift in society's attitude toward encouraging people with disabilities to remain active in public events. Does your church facility fully accommodate this growing segment of her congregation?

What other design barriers can you find influencing attendance during your church's past? Does facility change account for any of the sudden rises of attendance in your congregation's past?

Growing past an average attendance of 200 requires a congregation to radically change the way they relate to their pastor.

200 requires a congregation to radically change the way they relate to their pastor. The church with more than 200 in attendance attracts people who want the benefits of well-organized programs and activities for their families. Making this shift requires a large amount of energy, as well as the willingness to change.

Because churches, especially ones struggling with facility limitations, often lack the resources to grow past this point, a phenomenon known as the "200 Barrier" can be clearly seen on the American church landscape. This barrier begins to exert stress on the congregational life and structure as soon as the church begins to grow past 150 in attendance, and the stress increases dramatically as 200 nears. Until the church exceeds an average attendance of 225 there will be confusion as to what the pastor is expected to do and how important program staff are to the life of the church. The older membership will continue to voice a preference for how things used to be run and how nice it was to have everyone in the same worship service. This increasing resistance explains why so many churches rise to 200, then fall back. There is a hidden wall that they run up against over and over.

Similar barriers also seem to exist for a smaller church growing to 75 in attendance, and for the larger congregation approaching 1,000. Churches with fewer than 75 in worship tend to be governed by one family or group of interrelated lay members. As they grow, not only do they have to intentionally reshape the church to involve others in the decision-making process, but they must also gather resources to provide for full-time pastoral ministry. Churches approaching the 1,000 barrier have the paradoxical challenge of reorganizing themselves around small groups. If they can restructure so that the entire congregation participates in some family-sized fellowship group, then they can continue to grow. In order to be a megachurch, they must make all participants feel that they belong to a place where people really know them personally. Each of these numerical transitions creates such chaos and stress to congregational life that the next barrier is rarely breached without some application of a transition process such as this book outlines.

Another way to understand how size-identity imposes real barriers to growth in a church is to look at living organisms in nature. A microscopic organism can reach only a

Congregational Size-Identity

Church Size	Barrier Located	Church Identity/Clergy Status	Qualities/Structure
Small	75 in average worship attendance	**Identity:** One Happy Family **Clergy:** Pastor is part-time, or church may share a pastor with another church. Since church functions informally, they may not require their leader to be ordained.	Adds new members by making them part of the church family. Decisions are made informally by consensus, with chief family leader having veto power.
Medium	200	**Identity:** The Flock of a Pastor **Clergy:** Pastor is full-time and ordained. Pastor's most important attribute is the way he or she maintains contact with everyone.	Adds new members by relating them to the pastor. Pastor does most of the pastoral care and program oversight. May have many part-time and volunteer lay leaders, but there is a strong sense that everyone in the church shares the same objectives.
Large	1,000	**Identity:** Church With Programs for All **Clergy:** Senior pastor has managerial responsibilities as he or she oversees other clergy and employees. Strength of the ministry is highly dependent upon the quality of the program staff and how well volunteers are incorporated into the organization.	New members are attracted by programs that meet their needs. Organization is less structured, allowing different groups to have diverse objectives.
Mega	None that we know of	**Identity:** Join Us, Join a Small Group **Clergy:** Pastoral care is handled by non-ordained group leaders. May have a well-known, "marketable" preacher.	Because the church has high visibility in the community, there is a steady stream of visitors. A process exists to incorporate everyone into a small group. Church may be governed by a board of skilled laity, much like a large nonprofit organization.

certain size before it has to divide. As long as it organizes its life inside a single cell, the creature has a size limitation, a growth barrier. Moving into multicelled structures is a major step on nature's developmental ladder, and creatures who are beyond that barrier look different and function differently from the amoebae and paramecia below them. Likewise, the church undergoes a radical transformation when it grows from 50 to 100, from 150 to 225, and from 750 to 1,000. See the table on page 82.

Church Size and the Pastor's Role

Often when longtime members reflect on the church's past glory days, they assume that periods of growth were entirely the work of certain favorite pastors. They say, "If only we had a preacher like old Reverend Longtalker again, we would have the pews full." Accurately doing a chart of the church's statistics, however, may reveal a different story. Some pastors maintain church vitality in difficult times while neighboring congregations lose members. Other pastors ride the popularity wave of times in which church attendance is socially rewarded, but do little to prepare the church for the future. For many pastors, success in ministry is a matter of being at the right place (for them) at the right time.

It is easy to see how churches at different size levels require different things from their pastors. A pastor who is running between several small churches on a circuit does not need to be an expert on managing staff or developing programs. He or she does need to have a gracious, encouraging, and sincere attitude, because much of the work will involve encouraging the untrained laity to run the church themselves. If the pastor is a perfectionist, he or she will soon burn out because the people and the circumstances of small church life resist overmanagement. It is important to note that church growth is less likely to be affected by a pastor's preaching or other skills than by the relationships formed with the members.

Pastors in medium-sized churches will be under much closer scrutiny for doing ministry well. They often resemble the circus act where the clown spins a number of plates on top of poles. Since many aspects of church life are dependent upon them, they tend to closely identify with the congregation. As church attendance grows, they work harder and harder. Any personal weaknesses become a liability to the whole organization.

The larger, program-oriented church has come to understand that their senior pastor is but one piece of their total success formula. To grow, they need a variety of ministries to meet the needs of potential new members. Having a capable preacher in the pulpit goes a long way toward ensuring the quality worship services that the larger church craves. The trick, though, is managing each staff person's strengths so that the whole organization is improved. If the senior pastor can do that, then many of his or her weaknesses will be forgiven.

The megachurch usually has a star preacher as pastor—as well as a carefully orchestrated process for assimilating new members into small groups. Looking at the prominent megachurches, one sees long-term senior pastors who, while being exceptional preachers, are also visionary leaders of processes that quickly incorporate new attendees into the intimate life of the congregation. People who join these churches may have first come because they heard about the senior pastor in the media, but they stay because the large worship experience has led them to be a part of a small group.

When a church in transition is having a change of pastor, it is important to match the new clergy's skills and personality to the size the church plans to become. This is important whether the church is growing or shrinking in attendance. Most pastors are truly only comfortable in serving the church that matches their size-identity disposition. Few pastors have the self-awareness needed to bridge over as a church changes from one size to another. This is one of the valuable new roles being explored by interim clergy.

When a small church is growing toward becoming a middle-sized church, it needs to not only become more inclusive of non-family members in decision-making processes, but also discover a way to purchase more clergy involvement. The next size-identity stage for them will require having a pastor whose skills they admire.

In a similar fashion, a middle-sized church whose attendance has dropped below 75 can probably no longer afford its own pastor. The committee on pastor/staff-parish relations will need to work hard to retrain the congregation's expectations to the time constraints of a new pastor who divides his time between churches. The lay leadership that steps aside from the blame game and creatively pursues the best options for sharing a pastor will provide the congregation with a great service.

When a middle-sized church approaches the 200 barrier, care must be taken to let the senior pastor capitalize on his or her strengths. Hiring capable staff becomes a high priority. Not only does the congregation have to shift their expectations and look to staff and volunteers for some of their pastoral care, but the church leadership has to diversify, allowing programs to compete with one another for the congregation's attention. A pastor who insists on having his or her finger in every pie will be the death of this transition process.

By far the greatest pain is experienced by program-oriented, large-sized churches who are making the transition downward. Often these churches are in changing neighborhoods or regions of economic hardship. For them the shift is one of constantly cutting once-valuable ministries, programs, and staff because of finances. For this transition they need a senior pastor who provides a healing presence in a time of grief. The steps of this book are designed to help congregations reorganize to confront new realities gracefully.

For almost every church in America, the issue of matching clergy to size-identity is about to become vital. The cost of clergy compensation is sky-rocketing, largely because of the rise in healthcare costs. Educational expenses—many seminarians graduate with over $75,000 in student loans—and retirement expectations have raised the minimum compensation qualified clergy are willing to receive for their services. Many denominations are also facing a clergy shortage that is likely to become more drastic in the future. These factors force churches to make tough decisions about their size-identity sooner than they would want to.

The congregation with wise church leadership takes the time now to extend their church timeline. What size is the church likely to be when they receive their next pastor? If that future is on the other side of a barrier, are there things that can be done now to soften the blow? If the church is currently growing toward an upward barrier, what can be done to ensure the right leadership across the boundary? If the church is shrinking, will making an intentional change in clergy expectation now, enable other resources to be preserved and leave the door open for a better future?

For Discussion

1. Do you feel that there are layers of hierarchy in your local church organization? Which people or groups are out of the communication loop?

2. How quickly are newcomers given permission to participate in meaningful decisions?

3. How could your group intervene and improve the church's communication system?

4. What facility limitations are most pressing for your congregation today?

5. Which category on the size-identity table (page 82) best fits your current congregation? Where are you likely to be after the transition process?

6. Is it possible for a church to imagine itself as a different size from the size they actually are? What can you imagine about your church?

7. What implications does this material have for how your committee on pastor/staff-parish relations evaluates the performance of your pastor and church staff?

Chapter 18
Generation to Generation

Another way to view your church timeline is to see it as a succession of different groups and generations of people who each led the church through their own era. One church tells the story of how they were the chief church in their region for their denomination from the 1940's to the late 1960's. They always expected to receive one of the top preachers of their judicatory, and their laity participated in denominational committees. Then a denominational merger took away their status of being a big fish in a small pond. As part of a much larger regional judicatory, they began behaving more like typical middle children. Instead of being on the forefront of social issues, the congregation concentrated on developing their own programs. Instead of taking pride in the skills of their preacher, they began developing a quality music ministry.

The Ones in Power

Each generation takes the church in a new direction. If you sit as an objective observer at the typical church council meeting, you can often note the interplay of dialogue between three generations. There will be the elder generation, whose influence will one day pass from the stage; the middle, "worker" generation; and the new generation who may not yet feel that they have permission to speak. This new generation may not be particularly young, and in most mainline churches today they are approaching middle age; but they represent a fresh viewpoint that is outside the thinking of the current majority. The actual center of power for the meeting may rest in any of the three generations, or it may even shift throughout the evening depending upon the issue under discussion. The group that the senior pastor identifies with, that may not be his or her own age group, will be an important dynamic for the decision-making process.

Every transition in American life since colonial times has been marked by the interplay of three generations. When there is a crisis or rapid period of change, there always seems to emerge a respected elder statesman, who departs from the conservatism of his generation and provides visionary guidance. There is also a middle generation who are flexible and adaptive in their attitudes toward life. And there is always a younger generation who are idealistic and ready to make sacrifices, such as going off to war.[1]

The same configuration of leaders is often present in the church when a major transition occurs. The stability and wisdom of a respected member of the elder generation is often critical to the process, but it is also important that a nostalgic centering of power in the elder generation does not stall the process. Adaptive qualities and idealistic energy will be needed from the generations who are at the center stage of the decision-making process. Care must be taken that one generation does not just abdicate its leadership responsibilities to the others. While every transition requires a shift of power and influence toward younger, fresher voices, the dialogue between generations is an important part of church life.

> Each generation takes the church in a new direction. . . . The dialogue between generations is an important part of church life.

Generational Attitudes

Today's understanding of the various generations of people who make up our churches should guide the church council in long-range planning and decisions about continuing programs that are losing attendance. The following table provides simple observations about each generation.

Generations in the Church

The Generation	Defining Characteristics	Effect on Churches in Transition
GIs 1910–1927 (also known as Builders)	Civic-minded and dedicated, their values were shaped by the Depression and World War II.	They have contributed generously to keep the current ministries alive but may be reluctant to accept the need for change.
Pioneers 1928–1945 (also known as Silents)	They experienced the Korean War and the civil rights movement. They are prone to adapt rather than react. They are often unassuming and reluctant to take on leadership roles.	They have the ability to see both sides of every issue. May side with the elders in keeping the church from making progress.
Baby Boomers 1946–1963	Idealistic and demanding, they earned the title "the me generation." They are always busy and are often raising their grandchildren.	They have altered each social institution they have joined. As young parents, they insisted that churches have modern nurseries. Now that they are retiring, they look for flexible and interesting ways to volunteer their time to the church's mission.
Postmoderns 1964–1981 (Also known as Busters and GenX)	Disillusioned by a world that offers less opportunities for them than for their parents, this generation has disappeared from many churches and has few members going into religious work. It is hard to estimate how their loss will impact the future of the church.	Hesitant to trust and make commitments to institutions, they are waiting into their late twenties to marry or start careers. Many still live with their parents. They would rather seek guidance for life from peers than from authorities such as the church or Scripture.
Millennials 1982–1999	Civic-minded, this generation seems prepared to enter military service and make commitments to institutions.	They are seeking spirituality in many ways, but many of them do not have connections to the traditional church or the Christian faith.
Genomics 2000–2017	They will be shaped by the biotech revolution.	It is too soon to know.

Current Generations in Today's Congregation

Looking at the generations table provides a meaningful explanation for why so many churches are in crisis today. After World War II, the GI Generation, who were young adults at the time, brought their civic-minded attitude and their high energy for accomplishing things into the church. Like no generation since, they attended worship and strengthened congregations all across America. Their dedication made the 1950's and the early 1960's a great time for church building projects and the establishment of new congregations. Since they were also busily having children (creating a population boom, hence the Baby Boomers), attendance in church school skyrocketed. This expansive attitude also generated successful youth programs and campus ministries. The decade of the sixties saw unprecedented numbers of talented young adults enter religious vocations and mission work. The elder generations in the church at the time felt a deep indebtedness to the GI young adults for winning the war, and hence were supportive of the changes this generation brought to the church.

The Baby Boomers, however, had a more diverse attitude toward religious life. They were idealists, and they insisted that the church be relevant to social issues. When Baby Boomers encountered resistance from the more conservative GIs who were in power, many of them left the church and found an outlet for social conscience in newly formed secular mission agencies, such as the Peace Corps. Large numbers found that working seven days a week and climbing the corporate ladder was more meaningful and financially rewarding for them than participating in church. Still others found the church to be one more thing to drop out from as they fled from the "square" establishment.

Many Baby Boomers returned to the church when they began to have children, a new generation known as Postmoderns. But the Baby Boomers raised this next generation without the confidence in and appreciation for religious institutions that had marked their elders. Baby Boomers were perhaps the first generation in history to say that their children should make up their own minds about what they believe. Baby Boomers also had far fewer children; so church school attendance, which is the bellwether of a congregation's future, slumped. The late 1970's and 1980's were also uncertain economic times, so the children of the Baby Boomers entered a job market that had gone bust. This and other social factors led the disillusioned Postmoderns Generation to think of themselves as Busters. Since they inherited a broken world, they lacked the confidence to commit to religious institutions or even the institution of marriage.

As America entered a new millennium, the picture for many churches became bleak. The GI Generation's unusually high post-retirement income, as well as their great generosity, enabled them to financially support and keep alive churches with declining attendance, but this generation is now passing on. Coupled with escalating costs of clergy compensation (especially healthcare) and the high cost of maintaining the larger facilities built during the boom, many churches are between a financial rock and a hard place. To further complicate matters, the Postmoderns have failed to enter the ministry at the same time that the great wave of talented clergy trained in the 1960's are exiting to retirement. The prospect of being unable to find or pay for competent clergy is particularly traumatic for pastoral-sized churches (75 to 200 in worship attendance). Further, the Baby Boomers who have returned to church have shown a preference for the larger program-centered churches and megachurches. This, along with America's continuing population shift toward the suburbs, has placed small- and medium-sized churches in jeopardy.

What Generational Understandings Mean to the Church in Transition

To summarize, churches in transition need to become students of their own history. Charting the generational changes should make us aware that the unusual expansion that characterized the previous century is unlikely to return in the near future. The current generations are leading the church in a different direction. To keep the church unchanged and hope for better days is unrealistic.

The Postmodern Generation and the Millennials may one day return to church. They, however, will come bereft of religious instruction and biblical knowledge. Ancient traditions will have little meaning to them. They will likely need changes, such as contemporary worship and church structures that are devoid of hierarchy, in order to feel welcomed.

In the meantime, the pastoral-sized church (75 to 200 in worship attendance), which is the mainstay for many denominations, is in danger of extinction. In order to survive, some will transition downward and learn how to share their pastor in yoked or cooperative ministries. Others will make the courageous leap across the 200 barrier and become program-oriented churches. This challenge will thrust their Baby Boomers into full leadership roles.

Doing transition, rather than simply waiting to react to social changes, allows the church to rediscover the God who works through history. In generations past, the church has encountered eras that are as inhospitable as our own. In every time, however, God is faithful and good to the people who call upon God in trust. Rarely, though, does God answer their prayers by letting them return to the comfortable era that is past. Instead, God leads them, and us, through the wilderness toward what God has decided is to be for us the Promised Land.

Endnote

1 See *Generations: The History of America's Future, 1584 to 2069*, by William Strauss and Neil Howe (William Morrow, 1991); pages 80–96.

Tasks for Church Leaders in Step III

- Survey the congregation to identify what areas of weakness or constraints are limiting the church's growth.

- Clearly identify what measurements will be used to assess the church's progress.

- Identify what the church may have to lose in order to go forward—selling some facilities, dismissing staff, closing down programs, and so forth.

Chapter 19
Bottlenecks and Yardsticks

The book of Hebrews offers this encouragement to us:

> Therefore, since we are surrounded by so great a cloud of witnesses, let us also lay aside every weight and the sin that clings so closely, and let us run with perseverance the race that is set before us, looking to Jesus the pioneer and perfecter of our faith.
>
> (Hebrews 12:1-2a)

The Neutral step of the transition process involves two things mentioned in the Hebrews verses. First it involves throwing off the things that entangle us and keep us from running the race of faith as a church. To do this we need to carefully assess where the church is encountering a bottleneck that hinders her in the process of making disciples or meeting her purpose. Second, this step involves measuring our progress against new standards. The author of Hebrews speaks of looking to Jesus as the perfect score that everyone who runs the race of faith seeks to obtain. Where do we find new standards for measuring our church life? How do we know which areas need improvement? What are the measurements that will help us know if the church has maintained her focus on Jesus and is running her race well?

Neutral is a practical, nuts-and-bolts step in the process. There is an old Chinese proverb that goes: You cannot put a big load in a small bag, nor can you with a short rope draw water from a deep well. In the Neutral step we measure how big the church's bag is. Neutral is the pause between gears when we ask, "Which measurement is most critical for us now: the depth of the well, the strength of the rope, the length of the rope, the capacity of the bucket, or the amount of water in this hole?" Just as a cautious driver looks in the mirror for one last time, the Neutral step marks the last chance to be reflective before we shift into the action gears of the transition process.

A Story: The Church With Too Many Problems

A small rural church has just had a change of pastors. The outgoing pastor expressed a great deal of frustration about the nearly completed building project he was leaving to Reverend Young. Comparing the forlorn image gracing the church letterhead, Young thought the new glass doors and skylight greatly enhanced the church's narthex and created a welcoming entrance. "Don't you see it either?" the old pastor asked. "With only a little more effort they could have added a handicap ramp and used this project to solve the church's accessibility problem. As it was, they never allowed me to present my plans for serious consideration." As the new pastor listened further, he gathered that the church's greatest weakness was its structures. However, there were problems not only with the physical buildings but also with the committee structures and the processes that the church used to make decisions.

Next Reverend Young spoke to the chairperson of trustees, who had a different assessment. "Our chief problem is that we are not getting any new people." This person expressed optimism that the new pastor would "do a better job at preaching" and increase the church's ability to evangelize the neighborhood.

Next the pastor spoke to the lay leader, who complained that all the church workers were exhausted from doing too much. "We need some of the younger generation to take over." When Reverend Young settled into his office, he looked back over the church records and saw how much the previous pastor had accomplished in just a three-year stay. He had prodded them into a stewardship campaign to wipe out old debts, as well as set in motion significant improvements to the property. The outgoing pastor was also active in the area ministerium and fostered improved ecumenical relationships. Few of these efforts, however, did much to empower the laity.

Reverend Young was deep in contemplation trying to make sense of all these contradictory explanations of the church's problem when Bertha, the church secretary, entered his study. "What are you doing just sitting here?" she asked. "You go out and visit the shut-ins and the church will take care of itself." Was this the sage advice he was seeking, or did she just present him with another possible answer to where the church's problem lay?

Wanting to get to the bottom of this, the pastor scheduled an extended meeting with the chair of the committee on pastor/staff-parish relations, who thought that Bertha's comment was a bit simplistic. After all, "The shut-ins don't represent everyone in the church, and the old pastor did an okay job of getting around to them." When Reverend Young pressed him for his own solution, he responded, "I don't think the church has any major problems; we're pretty much a typical congregation." Young countered, "But worship attendance is down twenty-five percent from what it was five years ago. There has to be some reason why the church isn't growing."

Reverend Young might have been less concerned about the church's current slump if he had not recently studied how congregations function as a system. Each part of the system is affected by every other part of the system; and even the smallest problem, if not identified and dealt with, may have a negative effect on the whole system. Reverend Young was convinced that churches become ineffective when they fail to overcome the current problem or barrier. Identifying that restriction is difficult for even a skillful church leader. The longer that one is in a situation, the harder it is to see the forest for the trees.

Later that fall, the church council invited a denominational consultant to meet with them. This consultant suggested that they use an assessment tool to identify the weakest area of their system. This program included a survey to discover the bottleneck that was restricting the church's growth. In presenting this well-researched tool for assessing congregational weaknesses, the consultant warned the council that "your weakness will probably be the one you would never guess."

True to this prediction, the members of the church council let out a collective gasp when the consultant revealed that not having enough strong, loving relations was this church's chief problem. These church leaders had always thought of their church as being a friendly fellowship. The consultant responded, "You may be cordial with one another, but the test indicates that you haven't gone deeper to develop strong connections between your members." Even Reverend Young was surprised, but as he thought about it he could see how few activities in the current church's program did anything to build a closer fellowship. To grow, churches need a lot of love.

The results of the test also quieted the urge many people had to blame the church's lack of growth on the previous pastor's preaching. Having known some of the church's history, the consultant was able to share how the trauma that had led to their indebtedness before the previous pastor had also damaged some of the relationships they shared with one another. When the previous pastor led them on a stewardship drive, he helped them solve their immediate need; but the process was emotionally exhausting. Further, focusing on building projects improved one aspect of church life but did little to meet the congregation's need for deeper fellowship.

"Wow, I could have gone out and visited shut-ins all day and not have done anything to meet the congregation's real need," marveled Reverend Young. "What should we be doing now?" "Well," said the consultant, "for starters you need to be doing more things just for fun. Get together in ways that will give you a chance to get to know one another, and don't always be so concerned about your obligations as a church." The consultant also showed the church council how to appoint an implementation team (or Pilot Group) to provide the leadership needed to overcome its current weakness. The council was enthusiastic; this answer was so opposite to everything else they had tried that it just might work.

When a weakness exists, the growth and health of the church is affected. Churches often capitalize on their strengths, ignoring the area of their weakness. This creates a blind spot in church planning. Unless the church's current weakness is addressed, all other attempts to improve the church will have little effect. Each of the solutions that Reverend Young had heard as he searched for the church's chief problem was valid and valuable. At another time, or in another church, they might have been the right answer.

In a year, however, the church council could sense that it was time to reassess the church's weakest area. Taking the survey a second time, they could see that they had come a long way toward improving loving relationships. Surprisingly, many of their other test scores were also improved, indicating a change for the better in terms of the church's total health. This second test revealed that their current need was for the development of small groups in the church. This church, like every church, has many problems and limited resources, but working on one weak area at a time provides a method for assuring continuous growth.[1]

> Unless the church's current weakness is addressed, all other attempts to improve the church will have little effect.

For Discussion

1. What problems do people commonly mention when they discuss your church?

2. Do you find it surprising that churches vary in terms of their weakest area?

3. Consider the possibility of inviting one of your denominational leaders to work with your church to assess your strengths and weaknesses.

Endnote

1 For help assessing your congregation's strengths and weaknesses, and resources for addressing the needs, contact your denominational leaders. You can also look at the Natural Church Development materials provided by Church Smart Resources, St. Charles, IL 60174; www.churchsmart.com; phone 1-800-253-4276.

Chapter 20
Some Assembly Required

In order to transition into a healthier congregation, each church must develop a successful process for fulfilling its purpose and a competitive niche where its form of making disciples is needed. Analyzing what needs to be done to make the church's disciple-making process productive has been the focus of the first three steps of the transition process (Park, Reverse, and Neutral). Capitalizing on a niche in society where your particular church's disciple-making process is needed is the focus of the last step (Drive).

Moving From Neutral to Drive

Imagine your church as an assembly line inside a factory. The end product of this church/factory is people who are equipped and enthusiastic about living their lives as disciples of Jesus Christ. As we saw in Chapter 11, a church can be busy, but if it is not involved in the process of producing disciples, it has missed its reason for existence. Many churches are like factories that are filled with rushing, busy employees but producing little of their intended final product.

As materials move down a factory assembly line, certain functions are performed on each one in turn. If a critical machine falls behind, the whole production line is slowed down. One can often discover that a machine is functioning below par by looking out on the factory floor and noticing where unprocessed parts are stacked up. Chances are good that the process is being delayed at that location. Discovering where the bottleneck is in the church may require more investigation. Instead of looking for stacks of parts, we need to test for where Christians are failing to get something they need to become fully functioning disciples. When the church has a failure at one of the critical tasks needed to produce disciples, the workings of the whole organization can be derailed.

When entering transition, most churches assume that they have many problems, like the example given in Chapter 19. After all, they have reached a dead stop in the process of making disciples. That logic is, however, flawed. When we are lost, there is usually only one critical turn that we missed. When an automobile breaks down, there is usually only one component that is failing to work. When an assembly line backs up, there is usually only one workstation that is halting production. In the church, there is seldom more than one weak area that is in need of immediate attention.[1]

Just as an assembly process is only as strong as its weakest link, so also the church is only as effective as its weakest essential ministry. In the transition process, moving from Neutral to Drive is a matter of implementing the changes that will address the weakest area of the church. Sometimes these changes are dramatic and threatening. Successful transition may involve such radical acts as relocating the church facility or totally shifting the way the church does its ministry. Before implementing dramatic changes, the Pilot Group needs to be prepared to clearly communicate how the change relates to a weakness

> In the church, there is seldom more than one weak area that is in need of immediate attention.

that is preventing the church from reaching its central goal of making disciples.

Returning now to the analogy of the church being like a factory, we can see how bottlenecks spring up in various areas of congregational life. In order to facilitate discussion, this book has divided the church/factory production line into three segments. Each segment has its own characteristic weaknesses. Questions are provided at the end of each segment so that you may engage your small group in evaluating your church's performance.

The Front Door

Notice how railroad tracks lead to one side of a productive factory, providing a steady stream of raw materials to be processed. In the church, the raw materials are visitors seeking a new spiritual relationship. The children born into our fellowship and the youth who are drawn to our outreach programs are also raw materials that we hope will one day become fully functioning disciples. Few adults today, however, are currently attending the church they grew up in. To survive in today's transient society, churches need to find ways to attract new members who first attend as strangers to the congregation. It is by incorporating first-time visitors that a church assures sufficient raw materials to continue to function in the disciple-making process.

Just as a factory can have a breakdown on the loading dock where raw materials arrive, so also the church can fail to be welcoming to newcomers. Imagine your church as having a special front door that is used only by people who are new visitors to the congregation. If this door were somehow to become locked shut, how long would it take your church leaders to notice? One small rural church of about a hundred members kept accurate records of first-time visitors. It was discovered that only five visitors (two families) had attended worship over a two-year period. Of these five people, two became regular attendees and eventually joined. During this period the church also had one birth, and four youth were confirmed. Balancing the other side of the equation, the church also lost eight people to death and relocation. Looking at the statistics for both years, one would conclude that the church was healthy. Membership declined by only one percent, and the congregation did a great job in assimilating their newcomers. But the front door (strangers entering the fellowship) to back door (members leaving) ratio was four to one against this congregation. If this trend does not change, the church will run out of raw materials for making disciples in the near future.

Another pastoral-sized church of 350 members found that they had new visitors better than half the Sundays of the year. But fewer than one in ten of these families became regular attendees. Of those that joined, the majority were transfers from the same or a similar denomination. Having a reputation as one of the better churches of its judicatory was clearly not enough to provide raw materials for making disciples at this location.

What evil spirit has bewitched the front doors of these congregations to behave in such a way as to doom the church to diminish over time? In every neighborhood there are great numbers of people who are spiritually seeking. Most neighborhoods also provide a steady stream of new residents who arrive looking for a church to participate in. The small church above was located in a region of moderate population growth, yet for some reason it was failing to capitalize on the spread of suburban sprawl into its neighborhood. Many churches today are dying simply because they fail to attract their fair share of those people who are already receptive to the message and the fellowship offered by the church. The people who worship there each Sunday are oblivious to how uninviting the church has become to those who are looking to join with them.

As mentioned in Chapter 17, facility limitations are often the cause of front door problems. Something as ordinary as failing to provide sufficient parking or failing to mark the church lot in a way that enables visitors to find a space may seriously affect the church's productivity. Visitors may not know that it is the custom of the membership to park behind the office building that is closed on Sundays. They may also fail to notice the itty-bitty sign that displays the time of services. Imagine how likely a family is to return if they arrive at an empty church, only to be told that the posted times do not apply during the summer.

Some churches, like the mythical village Brigadoon, have disappeared from public notice for years. They are not aware that churches with high visibility also have high admission rates at their front doors. When was the last time something about your church appeared in the newspaper? Has the church made any serious investment in advertising? The most important form of advertising is the word-of-mouth contact that church members make with their acquaintances. Unless the congregation is actively encouraged to be inviting, the average church member will rarely mention the church or faith to someone who does not attend.

To be healthy, a church has to reach out in evangelism that is focused upon the spiritual needs of currently unchurched individuals. Simply presenting the gospel each Sunday is not enough to make becoming a Christian accessible to those outside the church. No matter how well the rest of the assembly line functions, a failure at the entry point results in a loss of production for the whole system. The church, likewise, cannot function without evangelism, high visibility, and an inviting exterior appearance.

> The church cannot function without evangelism, high visibility, and an inviting exterior appearance.

For Discussion

1. How difficult would it be for a new resident of your community to find your church, discover the times for services, park his or her car, and enter into a comfortable pew for worship? Ask a relative from out of town to attempt the process and give you feedback.

2. Does your church have a regular process for discovering the names and addresses of first-time visitors and providing them with a nonintrusive follow-up call, note, or visit? Note: If you are depending on the pastor to call on first-time attendees, you are sending the wrong message. Laypeople who drop by with a simple gift are perceived as evidence of a friendly church. Pastoral calls on strangers are perceived as evidence of a clergy-centered church.

3. Does the average member of your congregation feel that it is his or her duty to invite others to join them in worship?

4. Is personal sharing of faith throughout the week promoted and encouraged in your church as a thing the average Christian should feel comfortable doing?

5. Does your church have a sufficient budget line for advertising? Are there leaders who make full use of free publicity and programs that improve the church's visibility?

The Assembly Line (Nurture)

Following the raw materials into the factory, one notices how the first steps of the assembly line involve simple connections between small groups of components. In the church, nurturing new believers in church school classes and small groups is critical to their acquisition of the Christian faith. Christianity is, at its core, a small-group process. Jesus organized his followers so that the small group of first followers nearest to him (the twelve disciples) would each go out and form his own small groups and, through the small-group process, would personally transfer the Master's teachings to still others who would form discipleship groups. Since the content of Jesus' teachings involves love and healed relationships, the natural way to share this message is in groups small enough to teach by doing. For many churches the greatest transition that needs to take place is the full-scale integration of small-group fellowship into the religious life of the average member.

> Christianity is, at its core, a small-group process.

Today large churches are discovering that the only way they can transition past a thousand in average attendance is by dividing the entire congregation into units of about a dozen people and making small-group attendance a stated expectation for all who would join their membership. Meanwhile program-sized churches (two hundred to a thousand in worship) are discovering that simply offering quality programs is not enough. Every program must in some way encourage the process of disciple formation. The easiest way to do this is to link programs to the formation of small spiritual groups. The men's basketball team no longer simply uses the church gym; they also stop and spend time in prayer with each other before playing.

The rising importance of small groups to church life is a testament to the shifts that are occurring in society. The Baby Boomer and Postmodern generations are decidedly anti-institutional. When the church presents itself as an umbrella for small groups, it no longer looks like an impersonal institution to these groups. Further, the Postmodern Generation has a disdain for authority structures. They refuse to be preached to, but they will accept a gospel that is presented to them inside the peer-to-peer relationships of a small group.

In the healthy church there are always small groups stationed near the "front door" who act as additional entry points to the congregation. Providing space for twelve-step programs and support groups of all kinds keeps the church active in need-oriented evangelism. For the church of the future, the entry point for new believers may come through some outreach program or support group as often as through the worship service.

The important aspect of this segment of the assembly line is the understanding that forming an individual into a Christian disciple requires more than an hour per week in worship. The fellowship aspects of discipleship are not mastered in our childhood years, nor do we graduate from the discipline of working out our practical faith in the presence of others who pray for us and hold us accountable when we leave Sunday school. Churches who want to be successful in carrying out their purpose must have a commitment to establishing an attractive small group for each member to participate in.

For Discussion

1. How do small groups relate to the Great Commission in Matthew 28:19-20a?

2. What has been the trend for small groups in your congregation leading up to the transition period? What do you expect will be the case after the transition period?

3. How does pastoral involvement affect small-group participation? What happens to the church's dependence on the clergy if small groups are properly established?

The Shipping Dock

At the far end of a factory one sees trucks carrying finished merchandise out into the marketplace. At the far end of the church process, one sees people who live out their faith in the marketplace of the world and are unafraid to act as Christ's disciples. The final assembly and shipping area of the church is the most complex stage of disciple production. It seeks to enable each believer to put his or her faith into practice and to participate in the work of the church. In the healthy church one finds five traits on the shipping dock:

- inspiring worship

- widespread confidence in the power of prayer

- sacrificial stewardship

- the encouragement of each believer to discover and use his or her spiritual gifts

- personal participation by the laity in mission projects and outreach work

One also usually notices in growing churches that the laity feel fairly comfortable in speaking about their faith and inviting their neighbors to consider inviting Christ into their lives. A church with a weakness in this area will fail to produce competent, compassionate, and empowered disciples.

The point of this end of the process is to get products out the door. The employees of a factory can make the finest product in the world; but if they do not fill their orders, they will soon cease to exist. Until recently, many churches survived purely on the confidence that they were good at doing church. Today, with almost an entire generation lost to the church (the Postmoderns) and dramatic changes affecting clergy placement, churches are no longer free to live only for themselves.

Just as the shipping process is prone to mistakes and needs careful quality control, so also is this goal of congregational life full of misunderstandings and easy to get wrong. We often think of worship as something we do for ourselves or as an attraction for others to join the church. Church committees often become focused on whether worship is being properly led, and fail to ask if it is meeting the needs of disciples who are ready to go out into the fray. Actually, inspiring worship is important because it equips the people of God to live in the world.

Stewardship is another concept that is easily misunderstood. Church leaders often assume that stewardship is a necessary evil done to get enough money to run the church's budget. Stewardship is actually a process through which disciples position their resources in the flow of God's grace. Churches who fail to teach stewardship do not die from lack of money; they die because they fail to instruct their followers to place this important aspect of their lives under God's control.

Today it is critical that churches find a way to involve their people in hands-on mission work. The Baby Boomer Generation expects the church to be socially active. People no longer give to institutions because they feel guilty. They give today because they believe that the organization is doing good in the midst of the world. The church that cuts back on mission giving in order to keep more money in their own budget is like the factory that stops shipping orders because they do not want to pay postage. Churches who are facing financial crisis need to maintain support for those missions that promise "a lot of bang for the buck" because many members will stop giving if they think the organization is no longer doing good in society.

One of the things that transforms a person from being a spectator on the sideline of faith to being a fully participating disciple is the discovery that God has already equipped him or her with a spiritual gift or talent for some area of service. People are like puzzle pieces: They get a clear picture of themselves as members of the family of God only when they see that their own odd-shaped personality fits into the fuller work of the body. Spiritual gifts exploration programs in the church often generate incredible energy, for many Christians feel that they have spent years on the shipping dock without being given the permission to use the natural abilities that God has placed in their lives.

For Discussion

1. Which of these quality attributes do you feel is currently the weakest in your church?

    ____ inspiring worship

    ____ confidence in the power of prayer

    ____ sacrificial stewardship

    ____ discovery and use of spiritual gifts

    ____ personal participation in mission work

Today it is critical that churches find a way to involve their people in hands-on mission work.

2. Which of the following describes the attitude of your church members?

____ The church really needs money, so I give what I can.

____ If I am in church, I put X dollars in the plate. It is like dues that I pay.

____ Most of the money the church needs comes from a few big shots or an endowment.

____ If the sermon and worship service are good, I will give a little more.

____ Giving is how I say thanks to God and do my part for God's kingdom.

____ I give a percentage of my income so that I can be a faithful member.

3. If you measured your congregation's spiritual temperature, what would it be?

Cold   Lukewarm   Average   Simmering   Passionately Hot

Presenting the Weakest Area

At this point in the transition process it is important that the church council be aware of where the church's weakest area lies. The Pilot Group needs to diligently work not only to isolate the segment of the church's disciple-making process that is failing to keep up but also to discover the resources that are necessary to fully interpret the problem. They may need to take time to gather statistics and locate comparisons between your church and others before they make a public presentation.

It is okay to take your time with Neutral. It is not easy to narrow one's attention and become convinced that the barrier to the church's progress lies in just one aspect of the congregation's life. Often what emerges as the weakness is an area that was considered least likely when your discussions began. Time and prayer are important. The group is attempting to discern what may have been a diligently hidden truth about the congregation. Remember:

1. In the church, there is never more than one weak area that is in need of immediate attention. There will be church leaders who will immediately propose other areas that deserve attention. Dividing resources at this point will only delay the implementation of the changes the church needs to perform to move out of transition.

2. Where the weak point or bottleneck is varies from church to church. That is why programs that are effective in neighboring churches may fail in yours. No matter how much success a new idea has had elsewhere, it is not worth trying on your congregation unless it addresses your bottleneck.

3. It is not fair to assume that your church's weakest area is the pastor. Most pastors spend their ministries scrambling to meet the expectations of the congregation. Those expectations rarely have any correlation to the church meeting its purpose for existence. The variety of expectations communicated to the clergy also does little to enlist their support in improving the church's weakest area. It is safe to assume that your church's weakness predates the current pastor. It will take a group effort, including the pastor's commitment, to develop a way to attack the church's weak area.

A church bottleneck or weakest area is like an elephant in the living room. Everyone notices the elephant when it first appears, but after a few years it barely gets mentioned. The bottleneck is an issue that everyone has skirted around for so long that it is no longer seen or spoken about. But once you step back and see it, you cannot stop seeing it.

Endnote

1 This is an application of the Theory of Constraints, which was developed by Eliyahu Goldratt for assembly line management. See *The Goal: A Process of Ongoing Improvement*, by Eliyahu M. Goldratt and Jeff Cox (2nd edition: Gower Publishing Co., 1993).

Chapter 21
Choosing a Yardstick

I n Chapter 20 we imagined the church as a factory constructed to produce disciples, thereby fulfilling Christ's mandate in Matthew 28:19-20a. Those who manage a factory keep close track of a multitude of sales and production figures in order to access the health of their business. The most important overall yardstick for managers is the bottom line, or the amount of profit the company received for products sold and shipped, minus expenses. A business cannot choose to ignore this figure. Other figures are also watched, but they each derive their importance from how they relate to the bottom line.

The church, thankfully, does not have a bottom line that can be measured in dollars and cents. Nor do we have stockholders or large numbers of employees who could not find better paying jobs in another field. But the church does have a purpose that can be measured: to go and make disciples of all nations. In this sense the church is a solely owned corporation (that is, a business that has only one stockholder) whose principle owner is Christ. The countless people who volunteer time and contribute sacrificially also have an interest in making sure that the church is fulfilling its highest calling.

Why contribute to or volunteer time at an organization that is not doing anything worthwhile? When a church is experiencing poor stewardship or a loss of volunteers, some attention must be paid to whether or not the church's achievements toward making disciples are being communicated, and whether the church is making progress toward fulfilling the task Christ gave to it. People want to know the bottom line.

The number of disciples "made" comprises many factors that can be individually measured but not easily combined. A local church's bottom line may include factors as diverse as

- the number of baptisms
- the number of refugees fed through the mission giving of the church
- the number of youth confirmed
- the number of volunteers engaged in active service
- the number of new people in worship

The number we really want to know is, How many people were encouraged to live a life of Christian discipleship by the work of this church over the past year? Unfortunately, this is a number that only God knows. But to maintain accountability with their membership, the church leaders need to choose specific measurements that indicate positive or negative movement toward the goal.

Measurements Reflect Goals

One of the marks of any organization is that different people become concerned about different measurements. Unless there is open communication and agreement about which

> The church has a purpose that can be measured: to go and make disciples of all nations.

numbers matter, the chances of anyone being satisfied become slim.

The church is often like a family that went on vacation. The father had three critical measurements: miles per gallon, miles between rest stops, and the maximum number of miles traveled per day. The only gauges he needed to consult were his watch and the odometer. Mom was interested in family comfort and the education of her children. She kept score by consulting an extensive list drawn from her tourist's guidebook. For her the trip would not be a success without visiting certain tourist attractions and making the children read the historical markers. For Bobby, the only score that mattered was on his electronic game. He cried foul every time his sister bumped him or his mother insisted that they look out the window. Susy had another set of criteria that she never shared. She became more and more sulky as the trip went on, and no one knew why. None of their measurements provided meaningful insight into how to plan the next year's vacation.

If measurements do not aid an organization in making improvements, what good are they? Many church leaders assume that the local church council has no choice about measurements. The figures that the pastor submits to the denomination on the yearly statistical report are assumed to be the only figures that really matter. It is as if Moses were told on Mount Sinai to measure the church's progress by the number of infants baptized, the number of members who joined, and the successful payment of all mission shares. Further, many churches have adopted the practice from the business world of reading the monthly financial report first thing at their church council meetings, as if this were the chief area of concern. The bottom line of profit versus loss is not the appropriate benchmark for an organization that is concerned about making disciples rather than making money.

Nickels and Noses

Traditionally we measure "nickels and noses"; that is, we seek for more money in the bank, more people in the pew, and more members on the roll. While all of these figures relate to a church's long-term survival, they do not communicate progress toward fulfilling the church's purpose. Further, these statistics tend to call forth nebulous guilt rather than action. If the number of new members who joined is down this year, what am I to do? Every pastor desires a better-looking statistical report, but why should the person in the pew care? What the leadership needs to begin searching for in the Neutral step is the one or two quantities or events whose numbers will tell us that we are moving in the direction that is right for us. What shall be our yardstick?

One church chose number of children sent to church camp as its yardstick for the year. The link between this statistic and the overall mission of the church to make disciples was communicated to the congregation in a variety of ways. Starting early in the fall, the congregation was invited to contribute to the camping scholarship program. Fundraisers and contests also enabled the children and youth to work toward funding more of their camping costs. Each Sunday in January, a different adult presented a short testimony during worship about how going to church camp had changed his or her life. As the time for registration progressed, a thermometer showed the number of children signed up. Volunteers were enlisted to drive the children to camp and to participate in repair work at the camp. As the children and youth returned from camp they were given time in worship to express their thanks to the congregation, sing camp songs, and tell stories. Several of the youth told that they had made decisions to become Christians while at camp. The next year, the congregation was excited about sending even more kids to camp. Not only was more money raised for sending their own children to camp, but scholarship money became available for underprivileged neighborhood children. These children, in turn, built up the church school and youth fellowship program.

Just as a rising tide raises all ships, choosing to measure and elevate the right aspect of church life can generate excitement and improvement in the church's whole process for making disciples. To repeat what was said before, the church leadership needs to think carefully about what it will measure. Unless something is presented on a regular basis to the congregation as a target for effort, people will drift and assume that the organization has no purpose. Further, when a church is in transition, measurements should be chosen that indicate progress against the church's weakest area or bottleneck.

Consider the following alternatives to fixating on the traditional "nickels and noses." Each of the figures below could be posted in a visible place before the congregation as it gathers for worship. Church leaders should tell the congregation why they believe that each statistic is important. How does this figure relate to the overall purpose of the church in making disciples? What target numbers will be reasons for the church to celebrate?

Churches with a weakness at the front door of congregational life could

- post the number of new visitors who have attended over the last four Sundays so that worshipers are aware that they should be inviting others to come and join them;
- recognize and reward regular church attendees for parking further away so that spaces are reserved for first-time visitors;
- seek to increase participation in programs that reach out to the unchurched, such as camp scholarships for neighborhood children;
- post the number of unchurched kids involved in youth recreation, vacation church school, or latchkey programs.

Churches with a weakness on their assembly line of congregational life could

- post the percentage of church members who currently participate in a small group;
- set a goal of sending more kids to camp;
- recognize those who complete courses such as *Disciple*, *FaithQuest*, *Christian Believer*, *Companions in Christ*, or *Witness*.

Churches with a weakness at their shipping dock could

- recognize people who make a commitment to tithe as a spiritual discipline for the season of Lent;
- recognize people who participate in volunteer work and mission programs. Seek constant increases in the number of people who are participating in an outreach program.
- post the number of people who have completed a spiritual gifts inventory or participated in an educational experience designed to connect them with their area of service;
- recognize the number of people who have become lay speakers, have entered the ministry, or are serving on denominational committees.

Like the search for bottlenecks in Chapter 20, engaging church leaders in choosing a new yardstick requires rethinking cherished notions about the church. We tend to think that if the church's bank balances go up, the church is doing better. But if we are not becoming better at making disciples or bringing healing to a world in need, our reserves are nothing but an insurance policy against the eventual death of the congregation. Our concentration on "nickels and noses" often deflects us from the weightier task of making disciples. Further, when casual attendees detect that the pastor and lay leadership are overly concerned about irrelevant statistics, they often respond by becoming less inclined to personally participate or to give. Constant harping about the budget digs a church deeper into its financial quagmire.

What shall be our yardstick? . . . The church leadership needs to think carefully about what it will measure.

Clergy Evaluation

The more church lay leaders think of the church as a complicated system, like a factory, the more they understand that no single person can fix the church. Nor is the church failing to be productive simply because the pastor needs to be changed. Pastors and congregations tend to become enmeshed, sometimes supporting each other's goals and sometimes operating in conflict.

There is perhaps no other occupation in today's workplace that is as loosely defined as that of a local church pastor. With the exception of a few hours of meetings each month and the weekly worship services, the large portion of a pastor's calendar and "to do" list is left vacant to fill in according to what the pastor feels is expected or needs to be done. For many pastors this is a process of seeing that the squeaky wheel gets the grease. A new pastor to a parish may receive a long laundry list of duties to fulfill because the former pastor did those things. The new pastor will also be told of additional duties to perform because the former pastor failed to do certain things that needed doing.

Rarely will a pastor be given the chance to work with the committee on pastor/staff-parish relations to create a reasonable job description that takes into account how his or her individual skills can best help the church, yet having the pastor working in close coordination with the committee on pastor/staff-parish relations and the Pilot Group can be a significant asset to a church in transition. The trick is to shift the church's expectations of the pastor so that the pastor's duties support the goals that are being identified by the transition process. During the transition, the pastor's skills must be brought to bear on the church's weakest area. The pastor must also be given permission to neglect those congregational expectations that do not support the church's movement toward healing.

In general, during the first half of the transition process, the pastor's role needs to support the listening aspect of the process. By showing interest, the pastor encourages the church to map their history and gain insight into the congregation's family system and decision-making process. The pastor plays a therapeutic role, not providing answers but encouraging the church leaders to ask the right questions.

Midway through Neutral and on into Drive, the pastor's role shifts to being a resource person in the congregation's exploration of ways to overcome bottlenecks and barriers to the church's development. The pastor's new role is to encourage the church leaders as they explore options and communicate their findings to the congregation. The pastor is not to be evaluated for what he or she personally does in this process but for what he or she is able to encourage others to do. As the church heals, the pastor shifts from being a therapist to being a coach.

During the transition period, the pastor has the additional task of doing all that he or she can to restore and build the congregation's spiritual energy and sense of self-worth. Planning and preparing inspiring worship that links with the biblical themes of transition (see Appendix, page 139) is a high priority. The committee on pastor/staff-parish relations should grant the pastor permission to let slide expectations that may detract from this essential task.

Employee evaluations in general can easily become a yearly exercise in fault finding. The church's interests will be better served if the dialogue can center on the ways this person's skills are being applied to overcoming the church's weakest area. For pastors as well as other church employees, making sure that every item evaluated relates in some way to the church's goals for the future prevents the yearly evaluation from being a fault-finding expedition.

The pastor is not to be evaluated for what he or she personally does in this process but for what he or she is able to encourage others to do.

Excess Inventory

In doing the measurements above, we are seeking to increase what the church is accomplishing. A more serious problem for many businesses is something known as excess inventory. This means that raw materials have been purchased and assembly has begun, but there have not been orders or sales for the goods. Bins of half-finished assemblies line warehouse shelves.

Almost every church faces a similar problem. Most churches have facilities that are underutilized. There may be rooms that are vacant except for one hour a week. There may be donations, often safely tucked away in memorial funds, that are not being used to meet the church's purpose. How do we view such excess inventory?

When a small business is beginning to fail, one of the mistakes managers frequently make is to count their excess inventory as an asset. They say, "We cannot be going bankrupt. We have all this product on the shelves." In the same way, a church may look at its large building and say, "We can't be missing our purpose. We still have this beautiful sanctuary." Savvy business leaders realize that inventory can impede progress. Anyone who seeks to protect inventory is not interested in growth. Getting back on track, for businesses as well as for churches, usually involves liquidating some form of excess inventory.

For some churches this means inviting an outreach group to make weekday use of the church's unused rooms. For other churches this means releasing some long-held memorial funds to address some current need related to their weakest area. For still other churches, this involves sharing an underutilized pastor or other church employee with another church, extension ministry, or mission work.

For Discussion

1. Take a few moments to list the assets of your church that may be considered excess inventory. These assets may be people, rooms, or funds. What is preventing the church from creatively using these items?

2. Take time, individually or as a group, to work through "Bible Study: The Love Yardstick," on page 106.

Bible Study: The Love Yardstick

1. Look again at this familiar passage of Scripture:

> If I speak in the tongues of mortals and of angels, but do not have love, I am a noisy gong or a clanging cymbal. And if I have prophetic powers, and understand all mysteries and all knowledge, and if I have all faith, so as to remove mountains, but do not have love, I am nothing. If I give away all my possessions, and if I hand over my body so that I may boast, but do not have love, I gain nothing.
>
> (1 Corinthians 13:1-3)

The apostle Paul is seeking to answer the question, What makes for a successful life? He presents here a series of accomplishments that people think will make their lives great. List these yardsticks that Paul says do not make for success.

Yardstick   **Person**

Look again at your list, and name a famous person who exemplifies each of the listed accomplishments or qualities.

What yardstick is Paul suggesting for making his life successful?

2. Look at the next verses and see how Paul develops measurements for describing love.

> Love is patient; love is kind; love is not envious or boastful or arrogant or rude. It does not insist on its own way; it is not irritable or resentful; it does not rejoice in wrongdoing, but rejoices in the truth. It bears all things, believes all things, hopes all things, endures all things.
>
> (1 Corinthians 13:4-7)

Love can be an overused term. How does Paul make it specific?

Being as specific as possible, develop a measuring system for several of these qualities for a typical week in your life. For example, [love is not] arrogant or rude equals the number of times I wave someone into my lane in front of me during rush hour traffic, and so forth.

3. Look back through Chapter 21 and at the verses that precede the "love" passage:

> Now you are the body of Christ and individually members of it. And God has appointed in the church first apostles, second prophets, third teachers; then deeds of power, then gifts of healing, . . . But strive for the greater gifts. And I will show you a still more excellent way.
>
> (1 Corinthians 12:27-28, 31)

In 1 Corinthians 13, Paul seems to be talking about his own personal measurement of success; but what organization does he really want to show the "still more excellent way" of love to?

Specifically, how would you apply a yardstick of love to your church?

Chapter 22
Proactive Versus Reactive

Neutral provides an opportunity for church leaders to examine what has prevented the church from moving forward in fulfilling its purpose for existence. It is a step that serves a limited purpose and precedes getting the church into gear. Some congregations, however, have so lowered their expectations that living in Neutral seems normal. Many churches have spent years spinning their wheels, their leadership locked in the attitude that the church is a victim of a world bent against it. They express this feeling of being out of control with an endless stream of becauses:

• Because we are such a small church, we cannot meet our bills.

• Because we are an inner-city church, nobody cares about us.

• Because we are out in the boondocks, we cannot get a decent preacher.

• Because the parents do not care, we cannot get youth to come to our programs.

• Because unemployment is so high here, we cannot give to missions.

• Because everyone is so busy, we cannot fill our church offices.

• Because most of the neighborhood belongs to another church, we cannot get new members.

Anyone who has driven in snow knows something of this feeling of being out of control. There is nothing more frightening than feeling your car begin to slide. You react, slamming on the brakes. The car stops going where you steer it. You find yourself stuck off the side of the road. You are convinced that the forces of nature have conspired against you and taken control of your car.

Yet there are many good winter drivers who safely navigate icy conditions year after year. There is nothing magical about their success. The novice winter driver reacts to the sensation of sliding by jamming on the brakes, locking the wheels and causing them to no longer provide any traction or control. The wise winter driver, however, keeps his wheels turning and focuses on steering with the skid so that he can direct the car's momentum to where he needs it to go. The experienced driver learns to plan his trip ahead; he makes gentle adjustments to the steering wheel, brakes, and gas pedal. He is proactive rather than reactive.

For the church, keeping control when circumstances are bad requires focusing on what is in their power to do. Jamming on the brakes and being reactive only worsens the situation and removes options from the table. Church leaders must learn instead how to explore creative responses to the changing circumstances. More importantly, they must undergo an attitude shift so that they see each changing circumstance as an opportunity instead of a challenge.

Focusing Our Attention

Self-help author Stephen Covey has written extensively about the danger that being reactive instead of proactive poses to individuals and groups. Covey also speaks about the importance of choosing where we focus our attention as leaders in an organization.[1] A group's discussion can either focus on items related to concrete actions that the group can take toward meeting their goals and objectives, or meander down an endless stream of wishes and complaints about things they cannot change.

Where we focus our attention is like the flashlight a mechanic uses to view the dark recesses of a car's motor. The mechanic may wish he could change the car's color or age, or the willingness of its driver to pay the bill. He knows, however, that he can only hope to fix the car's engine, so that is where he focuses his light. The less distracted he is by things that lie outside that circle of light, the more likely he is to accomplish his goal of repairing the vehicle.

The Pilot Group at one church found themselves greatly concerned about the economic impact of an impending factory closing in the community. Many people both inside the church and outside were in danger of losing their jobs. Discussion about these issues occupied much of the Pilot Group's time and threatened to derail the work they needed to do to aid the church in its unrelated crisis. One committee member finally asked, "Is there anything we can do to influence the corporate leaders to keep our town's plant open?" When the committee members answered, "No," he then pointed out that this issue was outside of where the committee should be focused. "The more we focus on the risk of the plant closing, the more we spin our wheels." Then he asked, "If in a year from now our church were healthy and the plant closed, would there be things we could do to respond to the needs of the families affected?" This question helped the Pilot Group look at what lay within their own power. They also saw that they now had an opportunity to influence the caring attitude of their fellow church members.

As the evening's conversation progressed, the Pilot Group began to see that their mission lay in improving the communication skills and spirit of cooperation within the church so that together they could respond to people in need. They began to talk about the people within the church who might have an interest in starting a food bank or a clothing resale shop. They also talked about donating space in the church to programs that provided career counseling. In networking with other congregations, they discovered that there was a local group lobbying financial and government institutions to extend loan guarantees and prevent homeowners from going into default on their mortgages.

While only a few of these many brainstorms actually panned out, when the factory did close, the church was in a position to provide real comfort to people in need. Further, when the church had to adjust to a drop in giving caused by a rise in unemployment, the proactive stance of the church leadership enabled the committee on pastor/staff-parish relations to reduce the number of paid church program and ministry staff without jeopardizing needed programs.

Diversity

Most congregations are facing changing circumstances related to cultural and theological diversity. The society around the church, even in small-town, rural America, is rapidly becoming more pluralistic. Church leaders have a choice: They can be reactive, forming a wall between the church and her potential new members; or they can choose avenues of grace and proactive inclusiveness.

A century ago many congregations were debating whether they could continue as distinct ethnic units, ministering exclusively to people of a particular heritage within the American landscape. Now there are few congregations who identify themselves as "German" or "Italian," and even fewer who have European-language services. The churches who sought to maintain an exclusive heritage are largely gone. The churches that proactively sought to redefine their identity in non-ethnic terms have found a broader audience and new members needed in order for the church to continue. Those congregations that have failed to reach out to the new residents of their neighborhoods, to add services in other languages, or to make their programs more inclusive in other ways will face extinction. They will succumb to the fate of all organizations who fail to remain connected to their neighborhoods.

The point is that a congregation cannot win by putting on the brakes and reacting with hostility to what is happening in society. The church needs to be attuned to and responsive to its location. Church leaders need to be aware that social change may challenge their current congregation's comfort zone. For the sake of their future congregation, church leaders must proactively plan educational events that will guide their members forward. The goal is not to make everyone happy, but rather to keep reactive people from dominating the church's long-range planning.

In regard to theological diversity, committees on pastor/staff-parish relations should be aware that with the pressures of reduced clergy supply and increased clergy compensation, theological compatibility has become less of a priority in matching clergy to churches. If church leaders are aware of specific issues that strike at the core of the congregation's self-identity, they need to actively communicate this in the church's profile. When a pastor does lead a congregation into new theological territory, church leaders need to be prepared to respond proactively, with constructive dialogue and educational events, rather than reactively, assuming that the denomination sent them the wrong person.

Further, local church leaders need to be aware that young, white males have been in the minority for most seminary graduating classes for the last two decades. When local church leaders choose not to consider a candidate because of gender, age, or ethnicity, they greatly restrict the field of those available to serve them. The church, by its reactive position, may unknowingly be paying a price in terms of the competence, compatibility, or suitability of the person they receive. Instead of rigging their pastoral search process for more and more disappointing results, proactive leaders need to do the difficult work of educating the congregation to be more accepting.

> A congregation cannot win by putting on the brakes and reacting with hostility to what is happening in society.

For Discussion

1. Is your own personal circle of influence growing or getting smaller? What about the influence of any committee that you are on?

2. Give an example from your own life of a situation that can be handled either reactively or proactively.

3. What changes have occurred in the immediate neighborhood of your church in the last five years? in the last fifteen years? in the last thirty years? What has the church done or how has the church changed in response to each of these changes?

4. Has your congregation become inclusive enough in their attitude to receive their next pastor, regardless of race, gender, or ethnicity? What educational steps are being taken to move the congregation in this direction?

Endnote

1 See "Habit 1: Be Proactive," in *The 7 Habits of Highly Effective People: Powerful Lessons in Personal Change*, by Stephen R. Covey (Simon & Schuster, 1990); pages 81–86. See also *First Things First: To Live, To Love, To Learn, To Leave a Legacy*, by Stephen R. Covey (Simon & Schuster, 1994).

Chapter 23
Cutting Our Losses

For everything there is a season, and a time for every matter under heaven. (Ecclesiastes 3:1)

Transition eventually leads to change. Change is not simply the addition of new things; it is also the passing-off stage of those things that no longer have a role to play in our lives. In our lives as individuals, we see change and transition each time we move our family to a new location, enter into a different marital status, or say good-bye at the graveside of a loved one. In each transition, something is gained but other things are lost or packed away. In the church, transition cannot occur without the loss of something: a name, a building, a pastor, an outreach ministry, a distinctive ethnic or theological character, a traditional way of doing things, the fellowship of a people always gathered at the same place and time.

It is said that people in Africa used to capture monkeys by placing several nuts inside a jar with a narrow opening. A monkey would be able to slide his hand into the jar but would be unable to remove his hand unless he dropped the nut he had grabbed. Many monkeys would be unwilling to release the nut until it was too late. Only the monkeys who were wise enough to let go could move on.

Many churches going through transition fail to emerge as healthy congregations because they refuse to give up something they need to release. Visitors will not join these churches; they can sense that the future does not lie with them. But there are other churches who do recognize that there is a time for everything and that their identity as a people of God is not contained within a particular building, ministry, or style of worship. They hold these changeable things loosely and are able to position themselves on the American landscape where they need to be in order to be a viable congregation. By their intentional act of release, they have made themselves a friend of change.

Two in a Valley

In the late 1980's two small churches in Valleytown struggled with transitional issues. They were of the same denomination but were of different heritages and were facing different issues. One church had a declining, aging congregation and was having difficulty receiving clergy who matched their conservative theological bent or who stayed more than a few years. The second church was located at a dangerous intersection, and while their building had charming architecture, it lacked adequate room for their growing children's program. When a parcel of land was offered to this congregation, they chose to move, recognizing that they would leave behind the location where they had worshiped for over a hundred years. The expense of building also meant that they would have to give up on their hopes of hiring a full-time pastor in the near future. As building plans progressed, a

> In the church, transition cannot occur without the loss of something.

delegation from the church met with the people of the first church and explored the possibility of merger with them. They said to the first church, "Neither of our buildings is adequate to house the new congregation we could become if we joined forces. Come merge with us and we will form a new church with a new name reflecting both of our heritages." The first church was unwilling to lose their building and their independence. To this day, they are struggling on the edge of survival. The second church, however, successfully relocated, expanded its ministries, and is attracting new members.

Downward Transitions

Not every transition results in the church becoming numerically larger or more financially secure. Not every transition period ends with a return to a positive trend in terms of nickels and noses. Some transition periods are successfully completed with plans for the church facility to be closed or the congregation merged. Transition does not promise survival for a congregation in their current state. It does, however, provide for an adaptation so that the spiritual offerings in a region meet the needs of the people who live there.

Sometimes a downward transition provides for a better fit by matching available clergy to the current congregation's financial resources, a worship facility to the current congregation's size, or a worship style to the current congregation's needs.

Downward transitions are not easy for leadership groups to accept. They are even more difficult to sell to a congregation. If you as church leaders have come to the conclusion that the change needed in your church will be perceived by many as a downward step, the following actions are recommended:

- First, plan a prayer vigil or designate a period of prayerful reflection. Invite people to spend time in prayer and reflection, focusing both on the current personal prayer requests of the congregation and on a brief prepared statement that portrays in an unbiased way the realities that the church is facing. Church leaders should approach this prayer time with an openness to the Spirit providing an answer other than the change they plan to present.

- Second, provide several opportunities for the congregation to be informed of what is being proposed and why. Those leading these informational presentations should be prepared to respond with patient sympathy to the feelings of loss that the congregation may express.

- Third, plan ample time for communication and digestion before bringing any matters to a vote. The congregation needs to know that the democratic process for making this decision will be handled fairly. They will also need to be assured that all of the alternatives they have proposed have been explored.

Upward Transitions

Changes in the upward direction are perhaps even more difficult than downward transitions because they involve creating a vision for growth with a people whose mind may be stuck on simply surviving. The average lifelong church member sees new people join the church and thinks, "This is good news; there will be less work for me because there will be more people to share the leadership offices and raise the money for the church expenses." This mindset does not take into account the fact that growth, especially when it is beyond a size barrier, means more sacrificing for the existing membership. Gaining new people invariably means expanding the facilities or adding program staff.

As a church grows, there is always a lag in contributions as the expenses to attract and keep new attendees outstrips the new giving that they provide. Almost every upward transition comes with a startling price tag. How to communicate and prepare people for this sticker shock will be the subject of much of the next section. Church leadership working in these situations will often find themselves reflecting upon Jesus' words:

> Whoever does not carry the cross and follow me cannot be my disciple. For which of you, intending to build a tower, does not first sit down and estimate the cost, to see whether he has enough to complete it? Otherwise, when he has laid a foundation and is not able to finish, all who see it will begin to ridicule him, saying, "This fellow began to build and was not able to finish." Or what king, going out to wage war against another king, will not sit down first and consider whether he is able with ten thousand to oppose the one who comes against him with twenty thousand? If he cannot, then, while the other is still far away, he sends a delegation and asks for the terms of peace. So therefore, none of you can become my disciple if you do not give up all your possessions. (Luke 14:27-33)

Jesus' words serve not only to reinforce the need for prudent planning but also to remind us that even positive acts in the direction of fulfilling our purpose as individual disciples, and as a church, involve costs. We must count the costs with a willingness to put our all upon the line.

Contemporary Worship

One form of upward transition for many churches is to develop a contemporary worship service. If the church's weakest area has been the front door of receiving new people, then contemporary worship provides a two-pronged attack. First it uses worship music that is closer to what many people are choosing to listen to in their everyday lives. Contemporary worship may be country and western, rock 'n' roll, pop, or heavy metal; but whatever form it takes, it pitches itself to what people are familiar with and attracted to the other six days of their week. The second prong involves making worship less formal and more accessible to people who are unfamiliar with or turned off by traditional worship language and form.

In planning for contemporary worship, church leaders have to take a bit of a leap of faith. They have to permit a form of church that does not look like church to them to arise in their midst. They also have to be willing to fund something that may not appeal to their taste. Further, they may have to wait a long time to see positive results and must be prepared for the chance of failure. There are many factors that can cause a new contemporary service to fizzle, and leadership does well to fully research the subject before diving in. Three issues will need to be fully thought out:

- First, can we fund the equipment and leadership that the new service will need?

- Second, what form will the new service take?

- Third, what effect will the new service have on the existing worship services?

Exercise: A Change Initiative List

The exercise on page 114 is designed for the Pilot Group in preparation for a presentation to the church council near the end of the Neutral step of the transition process.

This exercise can also be done by the whole church council or any small group in the church, provided that they are aware of the church's weakest area as established by the evaluation described in Chapter 20 (front door, assembly line, shipping dock).

Even positive acts in the direction of fulfilling our purpose involve costs.

A Change Initiative List

1. If money were not a problem, what things would you like to see changed in your church? (6–8 items. Leave room to add more items.)

   _____
   _____
   _____
   _____
   _____
   _____
   _____
   _____
   _____
   _____
   _____
   _____
   _____
   _____
   _____
   _____
   _____
   _____
   _____
   _____
   _____
   _____
   _____

2. Add to the above list any changes you can imagine that would improve communication and relationships in the church.

3. If a group of outside observers were to visit your church, what items might they add to the list? Add them to the list.

4. What things has the church tried to do in the past but failed to do, that should be added to this list? Add them to the list.

5. From the items on the list in column 1, create a shorter list of only those items that relate directly to the church's weakest area.

   _____
   _____
   _____
   _____
   _____
   _____
   _____
   _____
   _____

6. Working with the shorter list developed in number 5, put the items in a logical order in which they need to be done—first, second, third, and so forth—to make the greatest positive impact upon your church.

   First: _____
   _____
   _____
   _____
   _____
   _____
   _____

7. Are there still items at the top of the list developed in number 6 that you feel are totally unrealistic for the church to be able to achieve? If so, can they be broken into smaller items that can be tackled bit by bit? Before crossing any item off of your list, consider forming a task force to explore the issue and creatively come up with more realistic solutions to the problem.

8. Develop a final list of one to five items that you would recommend to the church council as change initiatives to be explored in the final step of transition.

   1) _____
   2) _____
   3) _____
   4) _____
   5) _____

Step IV
Drive

Tasks for Church Leaders in Step IV

- Study the facts that surround the implementation of any change.

- Focus on a stewardship program that emphasizes time and talent. (Or begin other actions to empower people to shift into new leadership roles.)

- Set policies that will limit the term in office and influence of people fixed on the prior way of doing things.

- Take whatever actions are necessary to overcome the barriers or constraints noted in Step III.

- Be willing to take risks, and prepare to welcome and recognize failure as a learning experience.

- Study biblical passages that emphasize people taking a "leap of faith."

Chapter 24
Taking Action

Are you excited about the changes proposed in the Neutral step for your church? Good! Now it is time to wake up and smell coffee. Meaningful change is difficult to start and easy to stop. This section is designed to provide the Pilot Group, the church council, and any other groups involved with implementation with insight into the challenges ahead.

Crazy has often been defined as doing the same thing over and over and expecting different results. In the church, especially after the chaos of trauma, crazy can begin to feel normal. At this point in the transition process, church leaders must choose to initiate something new. Resting on the comforting thought that some healing has begun to occur in the church is not an option. The congregation must be led to institute changes that address the conditions present in the church before the trauma that initiated the transition period. The church must emerge from transition different, even if this change at first feels wrong.

Transition is all about change. The previous sections of this book have been presented to help congregational leaders understand the changes that have arrived uninvited at the church's doorstep. Now is the time to change the church's relationship with change. In the Drive step, the leaders of the church choose to embrace change and make it an ally. They choose to act rather than react.

For every congregation going through transition there is a pivotal therapeutic moment. It happens the first time someone says, "Maybe the event that traumatized us (or the change that was thrust upon us) was a blessing in disguise." However tragic the difficulty that led the congregation to enter the transition process, the healing phase ends and the growth phase begins when the leaders start mining the silver lining of that dark cloud. It may take a year or more to get there, but at some time the church leaders acknowledge that the need for change preexisted the trauma. Those piloting the congregation into its Drive phase need to remember eight facts about change.

1. Being Better Is Not Enough.

The world is not really looking for a better mousetrap. Each new advance in science has faced an uphill battle for acceptance. Few technological improvements are overnight success stories. Some improvements are like the Dvorak typewriter keyboard, which failed to displace the current "qwerty" arrangement of keys even though it showed a significant improvement in typing speed. The fact that something is significantly better than what exists is not enough to convince a majority of people to adopt the change.

To make matters worse, the church is by nature a conservative organization. A person today who wants to change his or her life joins an exercise program. A person who wants to reaffirm traditional values joins a church. While saying this may sound a bit flippant, there are within every church a significant number of people who have made commitments to the organization based on hopes that it will not change. Stability, not innovation, has been the chief virtue of the current church.

This attitude, however, does not mean that change cannot happen in an established congregation, but rather that those who work for change need to lead wisely. Overcoming resistance will take communication (see fact 4) and intentional recruitment of spokespeople for the change (see fact 5). Improvements do not sell themselves. Just because something is better does not mean that it will be accepted.

2. Change Means Loss.

For every improvement and adaptation to future realities, something currently valued will have to be sacrificed and relegated to the past. Just as Newton's physics decreed that for every action there would be an equal and opposite reaction, so also for every forward action something of equal or greater value (at least in some member's eyes) will be discarded to make room for the change. (See list on next page for examples.)

After a change has occurred and the new has become commonplace, it will be hard to remember what things were like before. In the midst of a change, however, many will find that the price is too high. Some, like Lot's wife in Genesis 19:26, will be constantly looking back. Others will be questioning if the church has strayed too far from her roots.

Part of the reason for doing the Reverse step was to give a broader perspective on change as a natural process. History is a constant process of change, and no generation can bind the next generation. In doing history, we the living give a place of honor to past generations, even as we prepare to move beyond their particular vision for the church. It would be ungracious to leave behind an obsolete building without first giving honor to the people who sacrificed to build it. The fact that we are no longer able to use an item or that we are dropping a program or a way of doing things does not mean that we are not thankful for the service these things provided the church in their time.

For any action item that is proposed in the Neutral stage, there will be some serious area of conflict related to something that will need to be abandoned. In one church that was building a new sanctuary, the church leaders requested that the architect incorporate some of the old stained-glass windows into the new narthex and hallway. This token act did not prevent the new sanctuary from being laid out for the contemporary style of worship the congregation was making a transition toward, but it provided a much appreciated sense of continuity for the older members.

Those who lead change in the church should never soft sell the items that will be left behind. The church leaders must weep with those who weep (Romans 12:15), not discount their fears and grief about what will be lost to the church. Time must be provided to allow a sufficient number of people to support the action. Of course, because there will always be some who cannot bring themselves to let go of the old, a one hundred percent consensus in favor of change may not be possible.

3. Not Everyone Likes Change.

Imagine a committee of ten people gathered to consider a new program for your church. Before the idea is even presented, there will be one or two people who have a predisposition to favor it because they like trying new things. There will also be a few who will be prejudiced against the idea because they distrust anything new. Of the remaining six to eight people, three or four will quickly come on board if they see that the idea has the support of the people whom they trust. The remaining three or four people will slowly add their support if they see that the majority has adopted the idea.

These statistics mean that in any organization there will be a few who are ready to

New Action Considered	Familiar Item Left Behind
Adding a second worship service	Seeing everyone at the same worship service (Adding a third worship service is easier than adding the second, because the familiar feeling of unity with everyone at the same service has already been sacrificed.)
Beginning a major building project	The church being debt-free (Some in the congregation may have a hard time allowing the church to borrow money. The congregation should be made aware that having a mortgage is one of the costs of growing.)
Starting a lay visitation program	Having the pastor do all the visiting (Some pastors have a hard time giving up the satisfaction they receive from doing these visits. Some shut-ins will complain that they miss seeing the pastor, but giving laypeople who have spiritual gifts of compassion and healing a chance to serve in this way is so beneficial to the life of the church that this sacrifice is well worth the challenge that may be raised to its implementation.)
Starting an afterschool outreach	Luxury of church school classrooms being unused throughout the week; security that the church building won't be subject to additional wear, potential damage, and liability issues.
Church relocation or merger	The congregation's identification with a particular neighborhood and building (Memorial gifts given to the church, as well as meaningful furnishings in the building such as stained-glass windows, may have to be abandoned.)
Adding contemporary worship	The current music leaders' control over everything that happens in worship. On-stage presence as well as off-stage storage of equipment may offend members.
Adopting a mission emphasis or a critical stance on social issues	The congregation's notion that religion, politics, and daily life can be kept separate (Many will find this to be an uncomfortable new territory.)

jump on board before any details are worked out, just because the idea is new. There will also be an equal number of people who will fight whatever change is suggested. Church council members need to accept that they cannot make everyone happy. Even if a plan is well presented and has few drawbacks and many benefits, there still will be opponents, some of them angry. Building consensus is a process of allowing those who are pro-change to influence and lead a sufficient number to tip the momentum toward acceptance.

In every church there are progressive people who have the energy and the enthusiasm to explore new ideas. They may be any age, gender, or theological persuasion, but what is consistently true of all innovators is that they are scarce. Only two or three in a hundred have this mindset. In some congregations they are viewed as oddballs and are relegated to the sidelines. The church committee on lay leadership (nominations) should be intentional about seeking and placing these people where they can be heard, for the church's ability to adapt to change depends upon their input.

Every congregation also has a slightly larger group who are predisposed to embrace change and have the relational skills to build support for new ideas. These people are not change fanatics, but rather they balance caution and open-mindedness. These people also need to be carefully placed and given a role. They and the innovators together make up the members who are quick to adopt change, yet this combined group is still in the minority. The majority of the congregation waits to see where the people they trust stand on the issue. Winning the support of respected congregational leaders is always the key to making change happen.

There are two factors that can tip the majority in favor of a new idea: (1) the perceived trustworthiness of those who have adopted the idea and (2) the care with which the idea has been presented and all questions have been addressed. Good ideas do not sell themselves. Getting people to accept change is a process. It must be handled step by step. The first step is to win some trusted supporters. The next step is to let the endorsement of these people be known so that those who are more careful or skeptical will feel inclined to join them.

4. Communication Is Essential.

To tip a congregation in the direction of change requires a great deal of communication. The Pilot Group and the church council may have faithfully worked through the transition process, analyzed the statistical history of the church, discovered the weakness that is limiting their growth, and finally arrived at a particular change that needs to be implemented. Is the hard work now done? No. There are still a large number of people who need to be brought on board.

Each of the following things must be communicated:

- what is wrong about the current facility, program, or way of doing things
- what other avenues have been explored
- how the church council arrived at its decision
- that trusted church leaders support this change
- what the new change involves
- what the process will be for voting on the change
- what the process will be for implementing the change
- what the timeline will be for each step of the process

Tremendous harm can be done by failing to communicate adequately. When church leaders communicate only the action that is being proposed, people feel left out of the process. Some who did not participate in the Neutral step will not understand the need for the change. Others will want to know if all the alternatives have been explored. Everyone will expect that the timeline for acceptance and adoption of the change will proceed slowly enough for their questions and input to be received.

If the church has experienced conflict or any form of leadership trauma in the past, there will be a particular concern that the votes leading up to the acceptance of the change by the church council were taken properly and with sufficient consideration. Assurances will need to be given that due process will also be followed in any congregational balloting that is needed. Often, especially in congregations recovering a sense of trust, there will be more questions raised about whether the change was properly approved than there will be over the nature of the change.

Effective communication employs a variety of vehicles. Consider the following tools for dispersing information to a wide number of people:

- Organize field trips. One church that was doing a major building project organized a number of field trips to churches who had completed similar projects. Often these visitations were packaged with a nonrelated sightseeing event, such as a concert, so that those who had not expressed an interest in the building project were enticed to go.

- Involve the children and youth in posters, fundraisers, and contests. Explaining a change to the children of a congregation goes a long way toward dispensing information to the whole church. Youth involved in planning and fundraising not only provide valuable insight and energy but will also be listened to by their elders.

- Provide printed biweekly project updates. Single-page bulletin inserts can break a complicated change project into manageable pieces. Use large print, simple language, and plenty of graphics and illustrations to increase readability. Caution: Do not depend solely on such bulletin inserts or any other printed material to communicate your message.

- Use the Web. If the church has a website, devote several frequently updated pages to the project. Use links to connect visitors with other churches' websites that display similar projects. Also search for quotations and case stories that support the change.

- Use skits and dialogues. Do not be afraid to use skits (the cornier the better) to draw attention to aspects of the project or change. People are receptive to short dramatic interpretations of a project or needed change.

- Use as many avenues as possible. Repeating the same bit of text in the bulletin, in the newsletter, and on the church website is not a problem as long as the information is reformatted appropriately for each media. If something is to be read to the congregation, it should be short. It is better to serialize an oral message, that is, break it into a number of two-minute spots over the course of many weeks, rather than to take one worship service to present the whole matter.

- Use pictures and models. Some people are visually oriented and comprehend things better when they can see them. If PowerPoint projections are possible in the sanctuary, a series of short presentations during the announcements can have tremendous impact. Presentations about building projects should include slides or video shot at a similar completed facility. Even nonmaterial concepts can be presented visually. If the church is considering changing its leadership structure, a mobile of the new organizational structure (like the one done in Chapter 9) may be constructed and hung in the lobby.

In creating a timeline for starting something new, we usually underestimate the amount of time we will need to get everyone on board. Charting a generous timeline for communicating each aspect of a change is a big step toward successful completion.

5. Change Requires Trusted Leadership.

For many people, who is presenting a new idea is more important than what the new idea is. For a congregation to adopt a change, it will need the endorsement of several significant leaders in the church. Inviting a number of people to give short speeches in worship on why they have chosen to support the change will help adverse members sense that a majority is considering the idea.

The need for leaders who support the ideas does not mean that having a significant leader who is opposed to a project will prevent it from going forward. Many congregations have a prominent naysayer whose influence is thought to be impossible to challenge. If, however, the Pilot Group carefully builds consensus and does its homework in communicating the project, the effect of this negative person can be overcome.

For most congregations, it will be important that the person who leads the change not be someone who is thought of as an outsider. The pastor, unless he or she has served the congregation for more than eight years or is the founder of the church, will lack the acceptance to lead the change effort. Lay spokespeople whom the congregation trust and identify with must be chosen.

6. Change Requires Celebration.

When President Kennedy challenged the nation to land a man on the moon within a decade, NASA had to break that overall goal into a number of smaller objectives. Successfully orbiting a man around the earth became an early objective. When that objective was achieved, a great deal of celebration took place. Celebrating a number of smaller achievements built the momentum needed to continue in the decade-long effort to reach the goal of landing a man on the moon.

When church leaders attempt to tackle a complex program or a long-term project, care must be taken to break the goal down into a series of smaller objectives whose successful completion can be celebrated. If the goal is to raise $100,000, the first thousand dollars committed to the project must be celebrated.

Nothing creates success like success. In any project there will be those who are sitting on the fence, withholding their support until it looks like others have made a commitment. In stewardship campaigns, recognizing commitments as they roll in allows later pledgers to be inspired by the earlier ones.

Even if what is being changed in the church is not something that requires gathering popular support or commitments, the process of breaking the goal into smaller objectives is important. These short-range targets provide an opportunity for the process to be tested. Is the change we are proposing really going to provide the results we anticipate?

7. It's Not Over Until It's Over.

Surprisingly, many churches stop short of their goals. Church leaders begin to sense success in a change process; but knowing that what lies ahead will require much more effort, they lower their expectations and announce that the current achievements are good enough. A similar event occurred to the children of Israel as they were journeying through the great transition from Egypt to the Promised Land. They had escaped the Egyptians and fled into the Sinai desert. There they found a variety of oases, and the Lord provided the bread that they needed day by day. One of the oldest songs in the Bible celebrates this newfound freedom (Exodus 15:1-21). When the scouts Moses had sent ahead came back with the news that there were giants in the Promised Land, nearly all of the elders decided that it would be better to stay in the wilderness or return to the slavery of Egypt (Numbers 13:25–14:9).

Each time we celebrate the achievement of a critical midpoint, we also need to recommunicate and clarify the ultimate goal. It is surprisingly easy for people to confuse obtaining the first objective with completing the final project. It is particularly important to continually clarify the ultimate goal when the attempt is to transition a church toward a higher size-identity (see page 80 and following).

- If the goal is to move from being a small, family-sized congregation to being a pastoral church, then obtaining the money needed to hire full-time clergy is only part of the journey. The church must further set its sights on creating the needed level of program diversity and an average attendance in the 150-per-week range. To stop short of these

A *goal* is the final, long-range hope of a change process.

An *objective* is an intermediary milestone or completed task on the way to a goal.

goals is to risk the church's falling back into its old size-identity.

- If the goal is to move from being a medium, pastoral-sized congregation to being a larger, program-sized church, then breaking 200 in worship attendance and hiring additional staff are only midpoints in the journey. Church leaders must develop criteria for expanding the program life of the congregation until it makes maximum use of the facility. Going from two to three worship services is an objective needed to guarantee worship attendance in the mid-range of the program-sized church.

- If the goal is to move from being a program-sized church to being a megachurch, a media presence is not enough. The entire congregation must become incorporated into a small-group ministry program. Large churches are in a precarious place when they rest on the celebrity status of their senior pastor or the slickness of their worship program.

The long-term goals of the change effort need to be communicated often. While many people will first come to support a change because they like what a particular component objective will do for them, their ongoing support will depend upon getting them to see the whole vision. Care must be taken not to quit too soon.

8. Change Is a Learning Process.

What you learn on the journey is more important than the destination. This reality is true for each congregation no matter what the project. If the congregation reaches the goal designated by the Pilot Group but fails to grow stronger in trust and loving relationships through the process, the success is really a failure.

Jesus once told a shocking parable that describes the experience of many churches who manage to reach their goal without working to grow inwardly in spiritual strength and knowledge:

> When the unclean spirit has gone out of a person, it wanders through waterless regions looking for a resting place, but it finds none. Then it says, "I will return to my house from which I came." When it comes, it finds it empty, swept, and put in order. Then it goes and brings along seven other spirits more evil than itself, and they enter and live there; and the last state of that person is worse than the first.
>
> (Matthew 12:43-45)

Any initiative to bring about change in the church, must have the same educational emphasis as the transition process demonstrates. Jesus, in the parable of the unclean spirit, says that the end goal of religion is not to clean up a person's life. The end goal is to so unite a person in fellowship with God that he or she is no longer an inviting target for evil. In the same way, the transition process is not just about overcoming the trauma that landed the church in Park. It is an educational process that reunites the church with her goal of making disciples. Once she is busy doing her task, the church is no longer as vulnerable to trauma.

When church leaders seek to initiate a change in the church at the end of the transition process, they must continue to be mindful of the church's educational and relational nature. If a church successfully completes a building project but in the work of obtaining the congregation's approval of the project fails to build a sense of trust in the change process, the last state of the church will be worse than the first.

For many churches, reinstating the democratic process is an educational experience. When an item is voted on, care must be taken to ensure that all the concerned parties are present. They learn how to communicate each issue so that the fairness of the process is above reproach. To these church leaders, having tasted the transition process, the orderliness of the democratic process is more important than the outcome of any particular vote.

Knowing that what they learn on the journey and the relationships they form are more important than successfully making their objectives on time, church leaders become more relaxed and open to the Holy Spirit. Study groups, field trips, and prayer circles become integral parts of the church's response to trauma and change. The church learns to be proactive rather than reactive.

For Discussion

1. Remember the changes you developed for your church in the Neutral step. How does your understanding of each of the eight facts about change affect your plans?

   - Being better is not enough.
   - Change means loss.
   - Not everyone likes change.
   - Communication is essential.

   - Change requires trusted leadership.
   - Change requires celebration.
   - It's not over until it's over.
   - Change is a learning process.

2. Consider the energy and advance planning needed to effect change.

   - Where do the changes you have developed in Neutral fall on the table below?
   - We would wish for all of our proposed changes to be in quadrant I so that they would require less work from us. However, sometimes the most important work of transition implementation falls in quadrant IV. Are you prepared to not be discouraged in the process of implementing your changes?

	Easy Change to Implement	**Difficult Change to Implement**
Will Greatly Improve the Church	I. Low energy needed to implement	II. Moderate energy needed to effect change
Will Moderately Improve the Church	III. Moderate energy needed to effect change	IV. High energy needed to effect change

3. Return to the changes you have developed in Neutral. Break each change into smaller components. Ideally, some of the smaller change objectives would fall into quadrant I. Implement these changes first, then celebrate their successful completion.

4. In the last six months, how careful has your church leadership been to use an above-board process in making decisions? (Check the one that applies.)

   _____ Very Democratic. Every issue has been fully communicated and all parties given a chance to have their questions answered.

   _____ Somewhat Democratic. Most issues were well presented. There may have been a few people who felt left out of the loop.

   _____ Legally Okay. Every issue was properly presented and voted on, but little effort was made to include those who had opposing viewpoints or who missed the initial discussions of the issue.

   _____ Somewhat Undemocratic. Most important issues came to a vote, but dissent was discouraged.

   _____ Very Undemocratic. Every issue was decided before the meeting. The leaders led; everyone else was told to get out of the way.

5. What efforts have been made during the transition process to improve communication and the fairness of the decision-making process?

6. What additional efforts need to be made to improve the perception that the church is operating fairly and aboveboard?

Chapter 25
Shifting Power

I n the transition process, going into Drive always involves a shifting of leadership power. Yesterday's thinking will not solve today's problems, and listening to the same voices will not lead to a new future. Hearing from fresh voices is essential.

Term Limits

Many churches have some type of term limits written into their policies for filling church leadership offices. The United Methodist Church, for example, requires in its *Book of Discipline* that the nine members of the committee on pastor/staff-parish relations be divided into three classes so that after individuals serve for a maximum of three years, they rotate off of the committee. This system, when it is allowed to work properly, brings three new voices to the committee every year. Those who have just joined the committee rarely feel inhibited from asking questions since they enter a group whose "old hands" have only been at the job two more years than they. Since leadership of the committee is constantly changing, the group tends to adopt a more dynamic and creative attitude about its work. People are not given a chance to get burned out.

A church may want to consider adopting a broader policy of term limits to cover all administrative committees. If a large portion of church offices are held for a predefined period of one to four years, the lay leadership placement committee will have an easier time finding qualified leaders, because no job is seen as a lifetime commitment. Experienced leaders who want to serve the church will tend to make themselves available for placement on another committee. New approaches to problems discovered by one committee get carried throughout the organization as the leadership rotates. Further, space is constantly being made for new members to be placed on committees as existing leaders rotate off.

One drawback to term limits is that people who are passionate about a particular work or skilled in a task will rotate off in a few years. A distinction should be drawn between the church committees that are administrative (those who oversee a project, ministry, or decision process) and the committees that are work areas or ministries. Administrative committees should have term limits because their job is to aid others in being able to do what they are passionate about. In this sense, the trustees committee should be a small, formally organized administrative group with term limits. Instead of doing repairs themselves, they should oversee and direct a larger number of volunteers who serve as they have passions and skills to keep the church buildings maintained and beautified. A person may serve only three years doing administrative oversight but may give his or her lifetime to being part of another group that is passionate about the church landscape. This distinction allows the church to have the best of both worlds.

Committees such as the worship committee and the finance committee may be composed of a mixture of members who have term limits and those, such as the organist and the church treasurer, who are present because of their skills and office. Since both these committees actually serve to administrate an area of church life, though, care should be taken to have the majority of members, as well as the chairperson, be people with term limits. This keeps the individuals from becoming entrenched in positions of power.

Besides being largely comprised of people who have term-limited jobs, the church council should have a mechanism for incorporating people who are new to the church. Some church councils have a number of at-large members that make up one quarter to one third of the total council membership. These people are placed in rotating classes with three-year term limits and are selected with an eye to balancing the council to match the composition of the congregation. If the council is older than the mean age of the person in the pew, the lay leadership committee looks for younger people in filling the members-at-large category. This mechanism intentionally provides space to incorporate new members as well as to assure age and ethnic diversity.

Leadership Problems

Often in the transition process, the Pilot Group or an outside consultant will identify areas where the church leaders are not conforming to the policies suggested by the denominational guidelines. There may be a reluctance to run meetings according to a standard procedure such as Robert's Rules of Order. The keeping of minutes may have lapsed to the point that people who miss a meeting feel unable to contribute to the next meeting. Church accounts may not be regularly audited or posted in such a way that members may view and understand them.

All of these are symptoms of an organization whose leadership has neglected the care and maintenance of their own processes. In the church, the way a decision is made is more important than the fact that a decision is made. Those who hold leadership roles in the church need to be students of the church's organizational structure and make a commitment to work within that process. Just as the newly elected United States President is required at inauguration to pledge a commitment to uphold the Constitution, so also newly appointed church leaders need to pledge themselves to a system of democratic process.

Healthy churches have a mixture of formal and informal processes. The formal processes consist of a number of expressed policies such as the following:

- Pastor and staff salaries are approved at the annual meeting (church conference).
- Church council minutes are printed and distributed to council members the Sunday before the next meeting.
- New members to any committee are approved by the church council.
- All financial accounts are audited each January by a nonrelated auditing committee.
- The counting and depositing of the weekly offering is handled by someone unrelated to the treasurer.

Whenever a church's actual process for doing something violates either its own expressed policies or the denominational guidelines, a warning flag should go up. Has the standard policy been overlooked in ignorance, or does the motivation involve some desire to hide actions that should properly be made public? Is there sufficient cause to suggest a change of leadership?

The informal processes of a church are practices that may be unique to that congregation. They come into practice as a way to simplify the decision-making process and may be dropped whenever they no longer serve the church. The following are examples:

In the church, the way a decision is made is more important than the fact that a decision is made.

- The chairperson is responsible for beginning the meeting with prayer.
- Worship on the second Sunday of June will be led by the Men's Fellowship, and on the second Sunday of October by the Women's Fellowship.
- Children are eligible to become acolytes at age seven.
- Some committees make their decisions by consensus rather than by formal vote.

Care should be taken not to confuse informal policies with formal ones. Informal policies are by their nature nonstandard. There is no reason to expect any other church to operate by these rules. They remain in existence only as long as they prove to be useful to this particular church, and are subject to amendment in order to keep the church flexible and adaptive to change.

Most churches will discover during the transition process one or more leaders who need to be removed from their current positions. Sometimes these people have made too much of an investment in building their own power within the organization instead of sharing authority with others. Others, however, are simply too resistant to change to be of use in their current position.

Change-Resistant People

We noted in the previous chapter how some people are by nature resistant to change. Having such an attitude is not necessarily detrimental to leadership. It can help provide long-term stability in organizations. What is critical in the church, though, is that those who are change-resistant not be left too long in positions where they can block needed progress.

One church was blessed with an octogenarian gentleman who had chaired the ushers' committee for over half a century. His usual method of performing his duties was to post on the bulletin board a hand-scrawled list of the men he wanted to usher for the month. His church was seeking to transition into a larger, program-sized church and had identified the front door of evangelism as their weakest area. The Pilot Group wanted to see the whole greeting experience extended by the church out into the parking lot so that newcomers were having their questions answered as they were ushered to their seats. To do this, the church needed to increase the training and dependability of their ushers. Further, they wanted the people who were visible in worship leadership, such as ushers, to reflect the diversity that the congregation hoped to achieve. All attempts to add women, minorities, and youth to the usher rotation were resisted by this respected but entrenched church leader.

Not wanting to dishonor this gentleman who had given his life in service to the church, the leaders chose to do two things: First, they gently divided the numerous duties that this active senior was performing into two categories. They asked him to continue to perform some of the jobs that he had been doing as head usher, such as lighting the acolytes' tapers. The other tasks were to be part of a new position, Coordinator of Church Welcome, and he was asked to play a role in training this new person. This movement toward semiretirement from head usher was gently presented and negotiated by the pastor.

Second, a surprise honoring of this octogenarian was organized. His years of faithful service were honored and a special pin given to him as "Usher Emeritus." The gentleman was overwhelmed by the many kind words that people shared at this occasion.

Not every church will be able to wrest the leadership reins as gracefully from the hands of those who have held them too long. There will be hard feelings as people are asked to step aside from what they assumed to be lifelong posts. Other leaders will find themselves no longer able to exercise the same degree of authority after the church goes through transition and reshapes its ministry.

One church leader campaigned hard against a building project. When the decision to build was passed by a narrow majority, she continued to voice opposition to the fund-raising and construction process. While no action was taken to reduce her leadership role in the church, the natural process of change relegated her to having a smaller and smaller circle of influence in the church decision-making process.

Often people will say, "There is too much politics in the church." The word *politics* actually comes from the Greek and Latin roots that emphasize the fair participation of all citizens in the decision-making process. If through transition the circle of those engaged in church leadership becomes much broader and more inclusive of those new to the congregation, the political process is moving in the right direction.

For Discussion

1. Look at your mobile of leadership linkages in the congregation, created in Chapter 9.
   - Which areas of the leadership structure are most critical for successful completion of the changes developed at the end of the Neutral step?
   - Are there broken links or a history of poor communication among the leaders in those areas?
   - What has occurred over the transition period to improve communication where it was previously weak?

2. Are there people in leadership roles in your church who are by nature resistant to change? What can or should be done to prevent them from being barriers to needed changes in the church?

3. What positions currently have a term limit in your church leadership structure? Are the term-limited jobs in your church largely administrative in nature? Are there other positions that are administrative but do not have term limits?

4. What can be done to increase the number of new voices in the leadership of your congregation?

Chapter 26
Getting the Money

Many churches will discover that the changes suggested by the Neutral step come with a shocking price tag. Money may have been the reason the changes were not done long ago. Now that the church has come through the chaos leading up to the transition, the hopes of getting that funding seem even more remote. But finding the money necessary is a matter of applying a step-by-step process, just as the leadership has experienced in working through the transition process.

The good news is that in most cases the money for the change is already available. The bad news is that it is in the pockets of a congregation who is not yet willing to give it. If properly done, the communication effort that brings the membership to trust the project enough to give sacrificially for it will also develop new habits of regular giving. In most cases, the money raised for the change effort does not take away from, but rather increases, the congregation's routine giving toward the church budget.

Fund-Raising Consultants

Often, church leaders need to seek the support of a paid stewardship or fundraising consultant. The consultant's first task is to examine the church and provide an educated estimate of what the church is capable of raising. This estimate often surprises the church leadership because they are used to thinking in terms of meeting the monthly budget. Capital funds campaigns tap into a congregation's hope for the future, and so reach into a much deeper pocket. The consultant also teaches the leaders how to run an effective campaign and celebrate successes along the way so that the project gains momentum.

The other thing to realize is that money flows toward money. The Bible tells how the early church engaged in a challenging mission effort to feed the impoverished people of Jerusalem. People such as Barnabas first stepped forward and showed that they were willing to give sacrificially to the cause (Acts 4:34-37). Then many others, observing that these leaders were making generous contributions, chose to join in. Just as a snowball rolling down a hill gathers momentum and size, well-organized stewardship campaigns generate congregational energy and astounding amounts of money for change.

It is far easier to raise money for new construction and major renovation in one all-out effort than it is to increase the regular budget. For this reason, churches who wish to add on or to make renovations that will reduce future expenses, such as modernizing the heating system, do well to consider a stewardship campaign. Simply trying to establish a fund for future work in the church's routine budget rarely works. A one-time major stewardship campaign can also be launched to pay off debt or to fund endowments. These types of projects are harder to sell, though, and may need to be packaged with another needed improvement.

Many consultants lead churches through a process similar to the four-step transition process in order to obtain the funding needed for the congregation's dreams. When you

> Money flows toward money.

look at each of these steps, it is easy to see why an outside stewardship consultant is often necessary for the campaign:

- First, a careful examination is made of the top regular givers of the congregation. Often a reasonable goal for a stewardship drive can be estimated by assuming that many of these givers will commit an amount equal to their current giving toward the campaign if the project is well presented. A consultant will also be looking within the ranks of the already generous for the campaign leadership that work with him or her. The trick at this point is to identify those leaders in the church whose giving can serve as an inspiration to others for the duration of the campaign.

- Second, resources are produced that fully communicate the project and the goals of the campaign. The church committee members developing these materials are often encouraged to draw from the congregation's history to discover examples of similar sacrifices made in the past. The current generation is encouraged to see itself as doing its part, just as the saints of old, in building for the future.

- Third, for a designated period of several weeks, the church's entire attention is focused on study and prayer related to sacrificial giving. As this period progresses, each member of the leadership team shares with the congregation the decisions they have personally made in terms of a sacrificial gift to the project. Each person of the congregation is then encouraged to spend time prayerfully making his or her own commitment.

- Fourth, a special event is then planned for collecting the pledges and totaling the commitments. Time is provided in this final period to celebrate the objectives that the pledge drive has realized.

- Fifth, if the campaign involves receiving the actual pledge money over a period of years, a carefully orchestrated follow-up process is begun so that contributors are kept apprised of their progress toward their commitment.

Stewardship and the Regular Budget

Unlike the above major campaign, almost any congregation can substantially raise the funding of its regular budget without the help of an outside consultant. The trick involves two things: restoring the congregation's trust in the financial process of the church and moving the congregation away from guilt giving and toward proportional giving.

Most church leaders are unaware of how damaging the lack of trust can be to church funding. Congregations have the right to know

- that their giving records and pledge commitments are kept confidential
- that all church accounts are regularly audited
- that income versus the expense budget of the church is voted on and followed
- that funds are segregated to protect designated donations
- that mission funds are expended with a minimum of administrative overhead
- that denominational funds are properly assessed and paid

Wise church leaders develop a habit of routinely providing updates on this information to the congregation. Building trust is a long-term process. Communicating answers to the congregation's financial questions before they are asked goes a long way toward inspiring confidence in givers.

Leading a congregation toward proportional giving is an educational task. Many churches have gotten into the rut of trying to put more pressure on people to give as the

Leading a congregation toward proportional giving is an educational task.

church's expenses rise. This guilt motivation actually has the opposite effect. People begin to see the church as a bottomless pit always asking for more. The goal of good stewardship is to have people set aside a percentage of their income as a fulfillment of the pledge they have already made before God.

Each year, church leaders should encourage people to prayerfully examine their own giving as it relates to what God would want them to give. The standard of a tithe, or ten percent of one's income, is presented as a faith challenge that one can make before God, not as the solution to the church's problems. People give when they feel that it is the right thing to do rather than because they have been made to feel guilty.

By encouraging people to sign a pledge card in the fall, church leaders take a proactive step in solving future budget shortfalls. There is a sense of covenant created when the congregation promises to include the church as one of their regular, monthly obligations in the coming year, and the church leaders commit themselves to developing a budget with fiscal integrity. Instead of begging for money, the church reinforces the commitment that people have already made by sending them regular, confidential accounts of their stewardship.

Church leaders should also communicate how the church's budget relates to fulfillment of the church's purpose. People want to know that some part of what they give funds the disciple-making process of the church school. They want to know how the offering enables the church to be involved in a particular outreach to the community. Some churches have taken the step of presenting their annual budget in two forms each year. For accounting purposes, the church publishes a traditional line-item budget that shows how expenses fall under different administrative categories such as Employees, Building, and so forth. But in the interest of encouraging people to give, they also publish a mission budget. This budget shows the same total income as the traditional budget, but expenditures are broken down to reveal how each ministry or program is supported by the general giving of the church membership. In the mission budget, the compensation of the pastoral staff is divided between various programs of the church where they spend their time. In a similar way, the cost of the church office is proportioned to each group that uses the office. The additional work required to present this alternative way to view church expenses pays off by helping people see the connection between the money they put in the plate and the ministries that they appreciate.

A further service to the congregation is to provide the kind of records and information that will aid members in taking charitable deductions on their income taxes. If the church wishes to receive physical donations, such as building materials, food goods, or cleaning supplies, the church leaders must be prepared with appropriate forms on church letterhead verifying these gifts. Making people aware that these gifts are appreciated and properly recorded encourages this kind of donation. One church put a notice in the bulletin each December saying that gifts received in the church office on the last day of the year would be credited for the current tax year. This simple reminder paid off in making the church a frequent recipient of large end-of-year donations.

Finally, mission and outreach giving is highly dependent upon telling the story and presenting a face. One church regularly supported the neighborhood homeless shelter to the tune of a few hundred dollars a year. After the shelter supervisor presented the message one Sunday and was able to bring with her one of the former residents whose life was transformed by the ministry of the shelter, the church's giving to the cause more than tripled. Another congregation found its interest in mission work jump-started after several of its members returned from a two-week mission work trip to Haiti. Seeing a face and hearing a story takes the giving out of the abstract and makes it real.

For Discussion

1. Look at the changes envisioned during the Neutral step (Chapter 23: "A Change Initiative List," page 114). What would be the total cost of funding all changes?

   • What amount would need to be raised to move the church reasonably down the road toward making the most important of the needed changes?

   • What would be a good first objective in terms of money needed to begin working on the changes?

2. Do you feel that the goals examined in "A Change Initiative List" merit hiring a fundraising consultant in your church?

3. Would a one-time, all-out stewardship campaign be of value to your church? If a campaign raised an amount equal to your church's current budget, which of the goals could be funded?

4. Which of the following statements best reflects your congregation's current giving habits? (Check one.)

   ___ Most people tithe (give at or above 10 percent) or give above 5 percent of their income.

   ___ Most people think of their giving in terms of a portion of their income but may not yet be tithers.

   ___ Many people give a percentage of their income, but they are not the majority.

   ___ Some people tithe; the rest give what they can week by week.

   ___ Giving a percentage of one's income is not a common practice in our congregation.

5. What effect could increasing the number of tithers have on your church budget? How can you educate people to give a percentage of their income?

6. Have each of the following been communicated to your congregation in such a way as to raise their confidence in the financial leadership of your church? (yes or no) Are your members confident that

   ___ their giving records and pledge commitments are kept confidential?

   ___ all church accounts are regularly audited?

   ___ the income versus the expense budget of the church is accurately evaluated?

   ___ funds are segregated to protect designated donations?

   ___ mission funds are expended with a minimum of administrative overhead?

   ___ denominational funds are properly assessed and paid?

Chapter 27
Major Changes: Closing, Merging, Yoking, or Other

God gives every bird his worm, but He does not throw it into the nest. (Swedish proverb)

Every church that goes through transition discovers a new future, but that future is not always what was expected. Sometimes God calls the church to discover a whole new form of existence, or even nonexistence. One of the lessons of the transition process has been that a church does not have the right to remain where she is purely for the convenience of her current membership. In today's world of escalating clergy compensation costs and diminishing clergy supply, a church, no matter what its size or wealth, cannot justify continuing as an independent unit simply because the facility is a convenient drive for those who currently attend, or the sanctuary is cozy and cute.

- Many small churches today are facing the reality that they may soon have to close. Faithfully working through the transition process does not always provide new life to a dying congregation. A small church, however, is not small in importance if it provides a needed witness to Christ to people who would not otherwise be served. The question that needs to be clearly answered at the end of the transition process is, Are we trying to keep the church open because we are attached to the building, or do we have a unique ministry that no other church can do in our region?

- Many medium, pastoral-sized churches are now facing the reality that they can no longer afford to support their own pastor. Yoking with another parish or seeking some type of part-time ministry seems to be the only solution. This transition, however, may lead the congregation into a more productive ministry than they would have previously imagined, because now they are forced to work cooperatively with other churches to meet mutual goals. Many congregations are discovering that by sharing a minister, they have not just lowered expenses but have entered into a fruitful relationship with a sister congregation. Because these relationships reduce each congregation's dependency upon their clergy, they invariably increase the laity's awareness of their own spiritual gifts and ministries.

- Many churches of all sizes are finding themselves lacking the resources they need to continue. Seeking a merger with another congregation while there are still money and members to transfer may be a proactive approach to a worsening situation. In completing this merger intentionally, a church can honor their past while allowing themselves to be part of a brighter future. Actively seeking a good merger rather than stubbornly clinging to the past is often the sign of a people open to the Holy Spirit.

Sometimes God calls the church to discover a whole new form of existence, or even nonexistence.

Regional Ministries

One of the most important changes a congregation can undergo is to look beyond their own institutional survival and position themselves to be part of a larger mission that meets the religious needs of people in a geographic region. Just as personal computers have become tremendously more valuable by being attached to a network, individual churches are transformed by entering regional networks.

One of the most exciting avenues for meeting the religious needs of people, especially in rural areas, is for congregations to link together and form group ministries or cooperative parishes. These larger parish formations allow the local church buildings to be worship centers in a dynamic ministry that shares resources. Some of these groupings of churches share everything, merging finances and membership roles. Other groupings preserve the individual identity of each congregation while adding the larger parish as a networking structure.

The concept is to hire just enough ordained clergy to oversee a ministry that is largely led and operated by laity. A typical group ministry may have a dozen churches served by two ordained pastors; three part-time, trained lay ministers; and a number of lay speakers. A schedule is developed so that the sacraments are served and worship led at each place of worship. Some programs that individual churches may be too small to operate effectively, such as youth fellowship, are shared. Each congregation may maintain their distinct traditions, but good creative ideas tend to diffuse rapidly around the circuit.

Besides bringing the costs of clergy compensation under control, group ministries have a surprising record for creating long-term stability. Many congregations who were experiencing a string of brief pastorates before entering a group ministry find that in the group association, they have relationships with pastors and trained lay leaders that last for decades.

Cooperative ministries may also be formed not as a means to share pastors but as a means to share ministries and missions. One cooperative ministry operates a food bank and a clothing thrift store and provides space for a health clinic that rotates between several of the church locations. There would not have been sufficient funding or volunteers for any of the churches to do these ministries on their own. Each church has benefitted from the reputation that the shared ministry has as one of the most compassionate providers of human resources to this remote region.

Reconfiguring Clergy Use

Many churches will find that they cannot fully transition into being a healthier church until they make more efficient use of the pastor. Clergy who are chronically stressed impede the congregation's ability to stay energized. Clergy burdened with unrealistic role expectations are unable to organize the laity so that each member makes the fullest use of his or her spiritual gifts.

An ongoing task of the committee on pastor/staff-parish relations beyond the transition period will be to evaluate what church work they wish for their pastor(s) to do personally, and what needs to be carried by the laity. A specific plan must be drafted and presented for approval at church council. Often a component of this plan is a schedule that reduces the number of meetings the pastor is expected to attend. Control issues must be addressed honestly and a greater leadership role designed for laypeople and nonclergy staff.

Transition often means changing the number or form of clergy leaders that the church employs. In some situations, tradition and/or the presence of endowment funds have enabled a church to keep a level of clergy staffing that is neither appropriate to its size nor able to serve the church's purpose. Clergy serving these situations may make work for

Clergy who are chronically stressed impede the congregation's ability to stay energized.

themselves, thereby depriving the laity of their opportunity to use their spiritual gifts. Worse yet, the pastors may simply become apathetic. It may take a great deal of courage for church leaders to request a downsizing in the number of clergy serving a church or to seek to be yoked with another church.

For Discussion

1. Most denominations or judicatories have guidelines for the size a church needs to be to support a full-time pastor. Ask your denominational leadership what the recommended level of clergy staffing would be for your size church. Do you feel that your pastor is

    ____ undersupported and possibly underemployed by having too few people to serve?

    ____ properly matched in hours of service available to meet the church's needs?

    ____ overstretched by having too many people to serve?

2. What factors are unusual about your current clergy's employment? Is he or she, for example, required to spend a large proportion of time overseeing an outreach mission of the church?

3. Is your pastor given sufficient time and encouragement to promote the ministry of the laity and encourage volunteerism?

4. Brainstorm about what new ministries serving the needs of your community could be started if several churches combined efforts. (Develop a list of a half a dozen ideas)

5. Which neighboring churches might be potential partners for some type of shared mission work?

6. Which neighboring churches might be potential partners for some type of sharing of pastoral time or other resource?

Chapter 28
Overdrive

Only that day dawns to which we are awake.
(Henry David Thoreau, *Walden*)

Is There Life After Transition?

When you first learn to drive, or when you return to driving after a serious accident, your initial trips are at low speed and around the familiar neighborhood. There comes that day when you bravely pilot your car onto the interstate. Shortly after you merge into the swift traffic you notice a large green sign saying the name of a distant city and the mileage to that place. You say to yourself, "I could go there if I wanted." This is the point for the driver, and for the church, at which you shift into Overdrive.

Transition is rarely fully completed in the one-year or two-year time period that was agreed upon by the church council. Ideally, transition is not like a circle that closes but like a spiral that opens out to changes that church leaders have initiated, which in turn cause unexpected results that need to be adjusted by further transition processes. The church's learning, growth, and spirituality keep broadening as it becomes flexible and inclusive in its orientation toward new changes.

There are several marks of this ongoing process:

- People begin to talk again in nonanxious ways about the future. The budget may still be in the red and the facilities inadequate, but confidence has been restored in the church's process for making decisions. There is now faith that the answers for tomorrow's questions will come just in time.

- Church leaders develop an attitude of wanting to learn from the church's experience. Occasional failure becomes accepted as the cost of learning. Past history continues to be mined for current insights. Procedures and policies are constantly modified to prevent future traumatic events.

- There is an appreciation for new voices. Church leaders are constantly looking for better ways to assimilate new members into the church's work and decision-making process. Even outsiders are tapped for their different perspectives on church concerns.

- The Pilot Group is replaced by a similar learning-oriented committee that leads the church in long-range planning. This committee meets and thinks about how the church should keep on changing. They do research on the region's demographics and discuss how the church should market itself to the next generation.

- The congregation shares the church leaders' concern that the church remain true to her purpose of making disciples. They constantly look for new mission projects and for ways to cooperate with other churches in fulfilling the Lord's mandate.

> Ideally, transition is not like a circle that closes but like a spiral that opens out to changes that church leaders have initiated.

When the period designated for transition draws to a close, be sure to celebrate.

When the period designated for transition draws to a close, be sure to celebrate. Provide an opportunity for the congregation to thank the Pilot Group and the other people who have worked hard through this time. Post a chart showing some of the ways the original objectives for the period of transition have been fulfilled. Communicate in a positive way the still unfinished work that will bring ongoing changes to the life of the congregation.

Finally, be aware that much of this book can be returned to repeatedly for preventative maintenance on the church's system for handling change. Having come to grasp the over-all process, church leaders are now free to apply whatever component or step is needed to keep the church moving forward.

Appendix
Timelines for the Transition Process

One-Year Timeline Following the Calendar Year

Step 1: Park

Beginning soon after New Year's Day and running through Holy Week, this low-activity step focuses on healing. It gives the congregation time to adjust to the concept of transition and to recover from trauma.

Congregational Events

- Announce the year-long "Period of Transition."
- If there will be an interim minister, plan an appropriate welcome service and social gathering.
- Downplay holidays and annual church events during this period. Lowering expectations enables the congregation to catch its breath, and the church leaders to focus on the challenging study material of this step.
- If a new church mission statement is developed during Park, unveil it on Easter Sunday.

Worship and Bible Study Themes

The Park step focuses on the present. Choose Scriptures and worship topics to emphasize the God who is here with us now.

The New Year

- Faith in God who rules history gives comfort and courage. Times and seasons change, but the love of God does not.

  Scriptures: Psalm 46; Psalm 90; Psalm 121; Ecclesiastes 3:1-15; Romans 8:28-39; Hebrews 1:1-4, 10-12; Revelation 21:1-5

Interim Ministry

- Compare the special work of a consultant or interim minister to that of John the Baptist.

  Scripture: John 3:22-30

Epiphany

- Contrast the wisdom of the wise men with the folly of Herod. They were open to a new future, even though they did not understand what God was bringing about. Do we respond to changes with fear or awe?

  Scripture: Matthew 2:1-18

- Tell the story of the slaughter of the innocents to illustrate how trauma can play a part in God's greater plan.

  Scripture: Matthew 2:1-18

- John the Baptist prepares people to live changed lives following their new Messiah.

  Scriptures: Genesis 6:1–9:17 (Noah and the Flood); Jonah 1:17–3:3 (Jonah and the Whale); Matthew 3 (John the Baptist). All baptism stories can be told as transitional examples.

- Tell the story of Jesus's days in the wilderness as an example of how temptations did not deter Jesus from walking the more difficult road of transition. The wilderness element of this story can also be linked to the Exodus story.

  Scripture: Matthew 4:1-17

- The meaning of discipleship: The story of Jesus calling disciples illustrates that faith puts us on a journey without telling us the destination. Discipleship, like the transition process, is a learning experience. The congregation is now facing an uncertain future, but like Peter and John they must respond to the present moment and choose to do what the Lord asks, step by step.

  Scriptures: Matthew 4:18-22 (calling the first disciples); Matthew 8:18-22 (the cost of discipleship)

- The purpose of the church: It is important to lead the congregation to think about their purpose, both in this step and in the Drive step. In Park, the focus is on the mission that all churches are called to. In Drive and in the period after transition, the congregation will think about their own unique purpose as a church.

    Scriptures: Matthew 5:13-16 (salt and light); Matthew 16:13-20 (foundation of the church); Matthew 28:16-20 (the Great Commission); Acts 2:42-47 (the new fellowship); Acts 6:1-7 (leadership transitions for service)

- Transfiguration Sunday: The transfiguration of Jesus, that is, his "changing," enables the disciples to see what has always been true about him. The transition process invites us to use the things that are changing in the church to view the things that do not change about God. This is also a wilderness experience for the disciples.

    Scripture: Matthew 17:1-8

Lent

Break the wilderness experience of Exodus into a 7-week series that prefigures the passion of Christ. Transition will, at this point in the process, feel like a journey across the wilderness.

- Ash Wednesday

    Scripture: Exodus 1:8-17 (the trauma of slavery)

- Week 1

    Scripture: Exodus 3:1-15 (God of the past and the future)

- Week 2

    Scripture: Exodus 4:10-17 (God equips us for transition.)

- Week 3

    Scripture: Exodus 8:16-19 (Plagues and trauma can be big or small.)

- Week 4 (Communion)

    Scripture: Exodus 12:1-13 (sacrifice and transition)

- Week 5 (Baptism)

    Scripture: Exodus 14:15-31 (deliverance; Transition means leaving the past.)

- Palm Sunday

    Scripture: Exodus 15:1-10 (joy and worship in transition)

- Holy Week

    Scripture: Exodus 15:22-24 (dealing with bitterness in transition)

- Easter

    Scripture: Exodus 19:1-6 (eagles' wings and resurrection)

Jesus' Beatitudes (Matthew 5:1-12) and his teaching of the Lord's Prayer (Matthew 6:9-13) can also be broken into a comforting and healing message series.

Step 2: Reverse

Beginning soon after Easter and running until early June, this step focuses on the congregation's history and denominational heritage.

Congregational Events

- Celebration of the church's history
- United Methodist and other Wesleyan denominations celebrate Aldersgate Day, May 24
- Pentecost Sunday

Worship and Bible Study Themes

Easter to Pentecost

Preach a sermon series on the purpose of the church. Use Matthew 28:16-20, the Great Commission, and elaborate on

- Jesus' authority in the church
- the mission to all nations
- baptism and transition
- the unchanging Trinity
- the teaching component of discipleship
- the presence of Christ in the church

Other Scriptures related to the church's purpose include Matthew 16:13-20; Acts 1:7-8; Ephesians 4:1-16.

Mother's Day

Recognize women in church history and as agents of social change. Break from the traditional Mother's Day service and focus on the accomplishments of women who transformed the church to underscore the difficulty of bringing about change.

Scriptures: Luke 8:1-3; Acts 16:13-15

Pentecost

Have a church rededication service. Retell the story of how the local church came into existence. Connect the local church's story with the story of the early church in Acts 2. Invite the congregation to renew their membership vows. Extend this day's celebration beyond the worship service with an appropriate fellowship event.

Step 3: Neutral

Running through the summer until mid-September, this step focuses on barriers that impede the church's growth.

Congregational Events

- Reveal the results of the congregational survey.

- A midsummer picnic fellowship may boost the congregation's unity and energy level.

- If there is a change of pastors, plan farewell and welcoming services.

Worship and Bible Study Themes

Summer

A summer sermon series will provide a sense of stability and comfort during the transition period. The subtle message of the series is that even though individual people's attendance is hit-and-miss due to vacations, the worshiping congregation is still making progress and on a thematic journey.

- If the Exodus story was not used during Lent, use it now.

- Wilderness themes also connect with those who camp during the summer. The transition of taking down the old tent in order to move into a new house (2 Corinthians 4:16–5:5) is a beautiful and comforting metaphor. Jesus' challenge for us to be flexible enough to camp with him (Matthew 8:18-22) can be used to support the transition process.

- Other series ideas include
  — the fruit of the Spirit (Galatians 5:22-25)
  — the gifts of the Spirit (1 Corinthians 12)
  — Jesus' Beatitudes (Matthew 5:1-12)
  — the Lord's Prayer (Matthew 6:9-13)
  — How would Jesus evaluate the church? Several messages could be drawn from Revelation 2 and 3. Look at each of the seven churches of Asia Minor. Which problems does your church share with these churches? What promises does Jesus make?

Labor Day

Labor Day Worship can focus on how work is evaluated. Scriptures may include Psalm 90:17 (establishment of work) and Matthew 25:14-29 (parable of the talents).

Step 4: Drive

Beginning in September and concluding mid-December, this step focuses on the implementation of changes that will aid the church in owning her future. The increased energy of this time is used to bolster the congregation's confidence in being able to change.

Congregational Events

- Fall stewardship campaign

- Advent

- Celebrating completion of transition period

Worship and Bible Study Themes

Change

Many Scriptures support the value of being proactive and intentionally choosing one's future.

Scriptures:

- Numbers 13:17–14:9 (the challenge of Joshua and Caleb)
- 1 Samuel 17:32-58 (David challenges Goliath.)
- Matthew 9:18-29 (people who acted to find healing)
- Acts 4:1-20 (Peter and John choose to continue preaching.)

Jesus makes it clear that being open to change is a prerequisite for following him.
- Matthew 9:16-17 (new wineskins)
- John 3:1-8 (being born again)

Stewardship

Scriptures:

- Malachi 3:8-10 (the importance of tithing)
- Acts 4:32-37 (the example of the early church)
- 2 Corinthians 9 (pledges as prepared giving)

Advent

The Advent liturgy focuses on the coming of Christ and the changes Christ's new kingdom will usher in. The positive energy and orientation toward the future make this a great season for bringing the transition period to a grand finale.

One-Year Timeline Beginning Midyear: June Through May

Step 1: Park

From early summer until mid-September, this low-activity step focuses on healing. It gives the congregation time to adjust to the concept of transition and to recover from trauma.

Congregational Events

- Announce the year-long period of transition.
- A relaxed summer picnic fellowship may boost the congregation's unity and energy level.
- If there will be an interim minister, plan an appropriate welcome service and social gathering.
- Downplay holidays and annual church events during this period. Lowering expectations enables the congregation to catch its breath, and the church leaders to focus on the challenging study material of this step.
- If a new church mission statement is developed during Park, unveil it during the church history celebration in the next step.
- Labor Day: Tell the original message of this holiday as a way of helping the congregation see that the social change brought to our country by the labor movement was an exercise in transition.

Worship and Bible Study Themes

The Park step focuses on the present. Choose Scriptures and worship topics to emphasize the God who is here with us now.

Interim Ministry

Compare the special work of a consultant or interim minister to that of John the Baptist.

Scripture: John 3:22-30

Summer

A summer sermon series will provide a sense of stability and comfort during the transition period. The subtle message of the series is that even though individual people's attendance is hit-and-miss due to vacations, the worshiping congregation is still making progress and on a thematic journey.

- Some series ideas include
  — the fruit of the Spirit (Galatians 5:22-25)
  — the gifts of the Spirit (1 Corinthians 12)
  — Jesus' Beatitudes (Matthew 5:1-12)
  — the Lord's Prayer (Matthew 6:9-13)

- If the Exodus story was not used during Lent, use it now.
- Wilderness themes also connect with those who camp during the summer. The transition of taking down the old tent in order to move into a new house (2 Corinthians 4:16–5:5) is a beautiful and comforting metaphor. Jesus' challenge for us to be flexible enough to camp with him (Matthew 8:18-22) can be used to support the transition process.

The Purpose of the Church

It is important to lead the congregation to think about their purpose, both in this step and in the Drive step. In Park, the focus is on the mission that all churches are called to. In Drive and in the period after transition, the congregation will think about their own unique purpose as a church.

Scriptures: Matthew 5:13-16 (salt and light); Matthew 16:13-20 (foundation of the church); Matthew 28:16-20 (the Great Commission); Acts 2:42-47 (the new fellowship); Acts 6:1-7 (leadership transitions for service)

The Meaning of Discipleship

The story of Jesus calling disciples illustrates that faith puts us on a journey without telling us the destination. Discipleship, like the transition process, is a learning experience. The congregation is now facing an uncertain future, but like Peter and John they must respond to the present moment and choose to do what the Lord asks, step by step.

Scriptures: Matthew 4:18-22 (calling the first disciples); Matthew 8:18-22 (the cost of discipleship)

Labor Day

Labor Day Worship can focus on how work is evaluated.

Scriptures: Psalm 90:17 (establishment of work); Matthew 25:14-29 (parable of the talents)

Step 2: Reverse

Beginning early September and running into the new year, this step focuses on the congregation's history and denominational heritage.

Congregational Events

- Celebration of the church's history
- Reformation Sunday (last Sunday in October)
- Fall stewardship campaign
- Advent
- New Year

Worship and Bible Study Themes

Church History Day

Have a church rededication service. Tell the story of how the local church came into existence, and connect this story with the story of the early church in Acts 2. Then invite the congregation to stand to renew their membership vows. Extend this day's celebration beyond the worship service with an appropriate fellowship event.

Preach a sermon series on the purpose of the church. Use Matthew 28:16-20, the Great Commission, and elaborate on

- Jesus' authority in the church
- the mission to all nations
- baptism and transition
- the unchanging Trinity
- the teaching component of discipleship
- the presence of Christ in the church

Other Scriptures related to the church's purpose include Matthew 16:13-20; Acts 1:7-8; Ephesians 4:1-16.

Advent

The fact that God is in charge of history and has a plan is seen in the long preparation time for the coming of the Messiah. Paying attention to the ancient Messianic prophecies becomes a parallel in worship to the congregation paying attention to its own church history.

The New Year

Faith in God who rules history gives comfort and courage. Times and seasons change, but the love of God does not.

Scriptures: Psalm 46; Psalm 90; Psalm 121; Ecclesiastes 3:1-15; Romans 8:28-39; Hebrews 1:1-4, 10-12; Revelation 21:1-5

Step 3: Neutral

Beginning with Epiphany and running through Lent until Holy Week, this step focuses on the barriers that impede spiritual growth.

Congregational Events

- Reveal the results of the congregational survey.
- Epiphany
- Lent

Worship and Bible Study Themes

Epiphany

- Contrast the wisdom of the wise men with the folly of Herod. They were open to a new future, even though they did not understand what God was bringing about. Do we respond to changes with fear or awe?

  Scripture: Matthew 2:1-18

- Tell the story of the slaughter of the innocents to illustrate how trauma can play a part in God's greater plan.

  Scripture: Matthew 2:1-18

- John the Baptist prepares people to live changed lives following their new Messiah.

  Scripture: Genesis 6:1–9:17 (Noah and the Flood); Jonah 1:17–3:3 (Jonah and the Whale); Matthew 3 (John the Baptist). All baptism stories can be told as transitional examples.

- Tell the story of Jesus' days in the wilderness as an example of how temptations did not deter Jesus from walking the more difficult road of transition. The wilderness element of this story can also be linked to the Exodus story.

  Scripture: Matthew 4:1-17

Yardsticks and Bottlenecks

- How would Jesus evaluate the church? Several messages could be drawn from Revelation 2 and 3. Look at each of the seven churches of Asia Minor. Which problems does your church share with these churches? What promises does Jesus make?

- How is success measured in life? Scriptures may include Matthew 13:1-23 (parable of the sower); Matthew 13:44-45 (parable of different yardsticks); Matthew 25:31-46 (parable of final judgment); Luke 12:15-21 (parable of a misspent life); 1 Corinthians 13 (love as a standard); Philippians 2:1-13 (measuring by the standard of Christ).

Transfiguration Sunday

The transfiguration of Jesus, that is, his "changing," enables the disciples to see what has always been true about him. The transition process invites us to use the things that are changing in the church to view the things that do not change about God. This is also a wilderness experience for the disciples.

Scripture: Matthew 17:1-8

Lent

Break the wilderness experience of Exodus into a 7-week series that prefigures the passion of Christ. Transition will at this point in the process feel like a journey across the wilderness.

- Ash Wednesday

  Scripture: Exodus 1:8-17 (the trauma of slavery)

- Week 1

  Scripture: Exodus 3:1-15 (God of the past and the future)

- Week 2

  Scripture: Exodus 4:10-17 (God equips us for transition.)

- Week 3

  Scripture: Exodus 8:16-19 (Plagues and trauma can be big or small.)

- Week 4 (Communion)

  Scripture: Exodus 12:1-13 (sacrifice and transition)

- Week 5 (Baptism)

  Scripture: Exodus 14:15-31 (deliverance; Transition means leaving the past.)

- Palm Sunday

  Scripture: Exodus 15:1-10 (joy and worship in transition)

- Holy Week

  Scripture: Exodus 15:22-24 (dealing with bitterness in transition)

- Easter

  Scripture: Exodus 19:1-6 (eagles' wings and resurrection)

Jesus' Beatitudes (Matthew 5:1-12) and his teaching of the Lord's Prayer (Matthew 6:9-13) can also be broken into a comforting and healing message series.

Step 4: Drive

Beginning with Easter and concluding on Pentecost, this step focuses on the implementation of changes that will aid the church in owning her future. The increased energy of this time is used to bolster the congregation's confidence in being able to change.

Congregational Events

- Easter
- Pentecost Sunday
- Celebrating completion of the transition period

Worship and Bible Study Themes

Change

Many Scriptures support the value of being proactive and intentionally choosing one's future.

Scriptures:
- Numbers 13:17–14:9 (the challenge of Joshua and Caleb)
- 1 Samuel 17:32-58 (David challenges Goliath.)
- Matthew 9:18-29 (people who acted to find healing)
- Acts 4:1-20 (Peter and John continue to preach.)

Jesus makes it clear that being open to change is a prerequisite for following him.
- Matthew 9:16-17 (new wineskins)
- John 3:1-8 (being born again)

Stewardship

Scriptures:
- Malachi 3:8-10 (the importance of tithing)
- Acts 4:32-37 (the example of the early church)
- 2 Corinthians 9 (pledges as prepared giving)

Pentecost

Have a church rededication service. Retell the story of how the local church came into existence. Connect the local church's story with the story of the early church in Acts 2. Invite the congregation to renew their membership vows. Extend this day's celebration beyond the worship service with an appropriate fellowship event.

Longer Timelines

Eighteen-month and two-year transition periods provide an even greater opportunity to cover all of the material.

- Select the appropriate one-year timeline from the two previously suggested (following the calendar year or starting midyear). Modify the timeline so that the first three steps (Park, Reverse, and Neutral) cover the entire first year.

- Devote the second year to the final implementation step of Drive.
- Stewardship is likely to be a major emphasis in the second year. There are enough seasonally appropriate Scripture suggestions in the two sample timelines to provide material for two years.